The Complete
CHOW CHOW

by

L. J. Kip Kopatch

First Edition

HOWELL
BOOK HOUSE
New York

Howell Book House
Macmillan Publishing Company
866 Third Avenue, New York, NY 10022

Collier Macmillan Canada, Inc.
1200 Eglinton Avenue East, Suite 200
Don Mills, Ontario M3C 3N1

Library of Congress Cataloging-in-Publication Data

Kopatch, L. J. Kip.
    The complete chow chow / by L. J. Kip Kopatch.—1st ed.
        p.   cm.
    ISBN 0-87605-102-6
    1. Chow chows (Dogs)   I. Title.
SF429.C5K66   1988   88-12966
636.7′2—dc19

Macmillan books are available at special discounts for bulk purchases for sales promotions, premiums, fund-raising, or educational use. For details, contact:

Special Sales Director
Macmillan Publishing Company
866 Third Avenue
New York, NY 10022

10   9   8   7   6   5

Printed in the United States of America

To dear Whizz, my wonderful friend who has made
all of my experiences in Chowdom, both the uplifting and
the devastating ones, so worthwhile.

—Kip

Contents

Acknowledgments

THE AUTHOR wishes to particularly thank those individuals whose major contributions were so important to the content of this work: Paul and Minnie Odenkirchen, whose wealth of photographs depict Chows, their owners and artwork worldwide; Paul Davis, whose vast collection of old magazines, photos and Specialty catalogues, largely from the estate of Dr. Imogene P. Earle, proved to be invaluable; Clif Shryock, whose photographs cover dogs and fanciers both past and present; Denis A. Lewis who personally photographed Great Britain's most recent winners; Bill Atkinson, whose statisticians' committee reports were responsible for presenting a wide range of facts; Nancy Meisner, who offered the Canadian statistics; Mattie and Chet Kopatch, my parents who offered typing and moral support, and Debb and Jim Keen who put their obedient Chows through their paces for the chapter on obedience. To all other contributors, the author is extremely grateful for you to have entrusted your precious, sometimes irreplaceable photographs to her care for inclusion in this book.

A green and gold iridescent pottery model from the Han Dynasty in 206 B.C., with an
unmistakable Chow structure.　　　　　　　　　　*Freer Gallery of Art, Washington, D.C.*

1

The Origin and History
of the Chow Chow

IN SPITE OF Chinese Emperor Chin Shih's destruction of Chinese literature and consequently records of purebred dog breeding, archeologists and naturalists have determined that the Chow Chow is one of the oldest breeds of dog. From a green and gold irridescent pottery model from the Han Dynasty in 206 B.C., we see an unmistakable Chow structure.

Max Siber in his *Der Tibet Hund* states that in 1121 B.C. Emperor Wu-Wang received a four-foot high hunting breed, the *Ngao*. The Chow resembles this dog of Thibet, or Tibet. Laufer's "Pottery of the Han Dynasty" names the Thibetan Mastiff with its massive skull and stocky build as similar to the Chow's structure.

In Edward C. Ash's *Dogs—Their History and Development,* he describes how the Tombs of Cheops of the IVth Dynasty in 3600 B.C. contain artwork of the *Khufu* dog. This Spitz or Chow-like dog is shown attached to the chair of its master.

Chows have been unearthed by archeologists alongside their Barbarian masters. Two of these tribes, the *Jung* and *Ti,* described their hunting dogs as "enormous lion-like dogs with black tongues."

The regions we recognize as Mongolia, Sinking and Tibet were home to these Tibetan Mastiff-type canines. As opposed to artistic renderings of Greyhounds wearing a neck collar while hunting, the heavy-skulled, deep-bodied Chow types are depicted wearing both a neck collar and harness. This need for such control by the hunter lends to the theory of these dogs' sheer power.

While it is held by some that Chows were used for food and fur, the most likely dogs eaten or valued for their pelts were actually Chow crosses. Because the Chow Chow's distinctive blue-black tongue can sometimes withstand crossbreeding, what was really a mongrel being fattened for dinner could have been mistaken for a purebred Chow. Archdeacon Grey wrote of black dogs' and cats' flesh highly valued, especially young, black forelegs and paws.

Instead, the true Chow Chows were highly valued for political gains and favors by the Chinese nobility. The hunting abilities of the dogs were tremendous. Stalking tigers and bears with their relentless trot and attacking with their powerful jaw hold, the Chow was a formidable hunter of big game. His ability to pivot on his straight hindquarters made him an invaluable companion on deer hunts through thick brush. To give such a useful animal as a gift to someone assured a favor in return some day, it was hoped.

In light of the Chow's prowess as a hunter, the T'ang Emperor of the Yunan Province established an enormous kennel of them. He had ten thousand huntsmen assigned to the care of over five thousand blue-tongued hunters. Although primarily considered for hunting big game, the Chow was also useful for quailing.

Pulling sleds was not above the capabilities of Chows, nor was their instinct to herd cattle. As a guard dog, the fearless Chow knew no equal. Although a high-pitched yelper when chasing game, he would silently confront an intruder. His blue-black tongue and black mouth were nearly invisible in the darkness. Then, if he did take hold of his victim, he wasn't apt to let go.

While early man was partially domesticating the Jackal in different regions of the world, the Chinese were actually keeping in-depth *stud books,* or documented breedings. When Dr. Abshagen was allowed to enter a Lamist monastery during the Japanese occupation of Northern China, he found that the monks had been detailing their breedings since the 13th century A.D. This revelation was chronicled in his essay "The Blue Chows of Mongolia." Not only had this monastery kept a strain of "heavenly blue" dogs going unto itself, with rare outcrosses to other monasteries' stock, but it

An alabaster carving of two Foo Dogs who very much resemble Chows.

A very rare Milk Glass covered dish with a Chow, circa 1880, England.

had established a consistency of type. According to the doctor, he had been given a well-deserved forewarning of the Chows' temperament. He had a club handy as the peas-in-a-pod pack greeted him and his companion, an Army Major.

Given as gifts to visiting aristocracy and traders to the Orient, the Chow found itself in ships' holds combined with other types of cargo. Instead of being detailed on the ship's inventory check-list, the oriental bric-a-brac and mixed pickles were lumped together to be called "chow chow." The exported dog came to hold this term when he was unloaded in England.

In *The Book of the Dog* the author Croxton Smith writes of naturalist Gilbert White's 54th letter penned in 1780. It read ". . . my near neighbor, a young gentleman in the service of the East India Company has brought home a dog and a bitch of the Chinese breed from Canton; such as are fattened in that country for the purpose of being eaten; they are about the size of a moderate spaniel of a pale yellow colour with coarse bristling hair on their backs, sharp upright ears and peaked heads which gives them a very foxlike appearance. Their hind legs were unusually straight without any bend at the hock or ham, to give them an awkward gait when they trotted. When in motion their tails were curved high over their backs like those of some hounds . . . Their eyes were jet black, small and piercing; the insides of their lips and mouths of the same colour and their tongues blue."

The increased importation of Chows to England from China did not begin until about 1880. Exhibited as foreign dogs, the breed was called "Chinese Edible Dog" in 1882 and in 1884, the "Chinese Chow" or "Chinese Chow Chow." Finally, its namesake became "Chow Chow" or "Chou Chou."

B. A. Burroughs wrote of the early history of Chows in England. June 1893 saw Chows attaining their separate register and thereby being entitled to a separate section in the 1894 Stud Book. This helped matters, since the Chows had, up to this point, been lumped together with other foreign breeds. Names could be similar, but actually of unrelated breeds. For example, The Prince of Wales' Chow was named "Chang," but one "Chang II" was, in fact, a Japanese Pug.

The English Chow Chow Club formed in 1895 and held its first show that year. The standard for the breed was purportedly based on Ch. Chow VIII. He was a Chow of very good type, but reportedly nasty temperament.

Ch. Chow VIII, on whom the
original English standard
was based.

C.W. Faulkner & Co.

Ch. Pusa of Amwell, an important stud from Lady Faudel Phillips' kennel.

Ch. Choonam Hung Kwong with his mistress, Mrs. Manooch. This Chow had taken an all-breed Best in Show win at Crufts.

Ch. Lenming, son of Ch. Pusa of Amwell above (Eng. bred). Lenming was the great-grandsire of Ch. Choonam Brilliantine of Manchoover. Through early imports from England to America these dogs appear also in other backgrounds of dogs important in American history.

The Earl of Lonsdale (Lord Hugh) brought the first good Chows to England to be given to his relative, the Marchioness of Huntley, whose daughter Lady Granville Gordon kept the strain alive. Her efforts enabled Lady Faudel Phillips and her mother to produce the first English-bred Chow champion, Ch. Blue Blood. Her famous Amwell Chow Kennel, active and most influential to the fancy for more than fifty years, eventually was passed on to Her Ladyship's daughter, the Countess of Kilmorey. She, unfortunately, gave up breeding after many discouraging setbacks.

In the late nineteenth century, Mrs. Scaramongo and her Kwhy Kennel became known, particularly with Ch. Red Craze. Lady Faudel Phillips' stud, Ch. Pusa of Amwell, in turn sired another important Chow, Ch. Pu Yi of Amwell. The Rochow Kennels of Mr. C. D. Rotch had Champions Rochow Dragoon and Rochow Adjutant. Mrs. Manooch's Ch. Choonam Hung Kwong, Ch. Choonam Brilliantina and Ch. Choonam Brilliantine were very famous, the last especially so. Brilliantine was exported to the United States for the then unheard of sum of 1,800 pounds sterling, about ten thousand dollars, to his new owner, Mrs. Earl Hoover.

Early into the twentieth century, further exportation to the United States, Belgium, France and other countries was done by the English breeders.

2

The Chow Chow
Comes to America

As CHOW CHOWS found their way into America, their exhibition remained infrequent. In an article by Charles G. Hopton, a Chow named Lager Beer is said to have been shown in 1880. However, according to another breed authority, Mrs. Baer, the earliest traceable show specimen seems to be Takya who appeared in 1890. In 1893, supposed Chow exhibits were reported at shows on both coasts. Three Chows were shown in 1896, four in 1897 and one in 1898.

Finally, along came the enthusiastic Dr. and Mrs. Henry Jarrett. After establishing their kennel in 1901, they actively campaigned Yen How in 1902 and 1903. In 1905, a pair of their Chows, Ch. Red Idol and Illswanga, won Best Brace in Show at Philadelphia. The Jarretts were instrumental in helping to organize the Chow Chow Club, the breed's Parent Club, in 1906.

Mrs. Charles E. Proctor's Blue Dragon Kennel was founded in 1904. In 1905, an English import of hers, Chinese Chum, became the first champion Chow Chow in America. His kennelmate Night of Asia joined him in championship status later that year.

The veterinarian Dr. Henry Jarrett and his wife were early American exhibitors and helped to found the Chow Chow Club, Inc.

The English import, Ch. Chinese Chum, the first champion Chow Chow in America.

CH. LU CHENG

CH. CHOP SUEY

CH. YUEY

CH. LEDGELAND'S SANCHO

CH. SUM SULTAN

American-bred champions, a distinction advertised as American kennels competed with English-bred dogs.

Ch. Win Sum Min T'sing was acclaimed as the top foundation sire in America. Mrs. Atherton Foster Messmore, The Sum Kennel, bred the dog who lived from 1912–1925 and sired Son of Min T'sing.

Ch. Son of Min T'sing

The Ledgelands Kennel of Mr. and Mrs. David Wagstaff had high success in breeding and showing. He was the delegate to The American Kennel Club for many years and she, the president of the Parent Club. Noted Champions were Sancho and Solo Chink.

Widely acclaimed by breed authorities as the top foundation sire in America was Ch. Win Sum Min T'sing. He was bred by the Winsum Kennels of Mr. Franklin Hutton whose daughter Barbara was heiress to the Woolworth millions. As a rule of thumb, basically the wealthy and well-to-do were the early patrons of the breed.

Mr. John Z. Adams was known for his homebred Ch. Lord Cholmondeley, as was Adnah Neyhart, Coassock Kennel, for Ch. Yuey. Dorothy White, formerly Mrs. Earl Hoover, Manchoover, had the great Brilliantine who was a top stud and show dog here after his importation from England.

Based on imported English stock, the Greenacre Kennel of the E. K. Lincolns was one of the most successful at the shows. Ch. Greenacre The Great Smut was one of their better known dogs.

The World War I years slowed breeding and exhibiting down. However, rivalries continued to abound, as homebred-versus-import theories were argued.

In the 1920's, a Chow in the White House with President Calvin Coolidge probably added to the general public's sudden interest in this unique breed. The numbers of Chows continued to swell through the twenties and into the thirties. This period of mass exploitation of the breed contributed to the Chow's unfair label as a vicious dog. People who were intent only on making a quick dollar on the much in demand dogs had no concern for taking the time to properly socialize or breed the Chow. The resultant ill-tempered and otherwise unfit specimens soon gave the Chow breed in general a black eye. The fly-by-nighters who had done their damage could no longer find a market for their stock and therefore departed. Only true lovers and caretakers of the breed were willing to try and pick up the pieces.

The Sum Kennel of Virginia Waller Messmore, formerly Mrs. Edward Cecil Waller, lasted more than two decades. Her Ch. Win Sum Min T'sing and his son, Ch. Sum Sultan were reknowned.

During the thirties, Mrs. L. W. Bonney of the Tally-Ho Dalmatians fame found exceptional success with Chows as well. Mrs. W. O. Penney, Clairedale, produced the great Ch. Clairedale Son Too, sired by Ch. Son of Min T'sing. The Mac Farlands' Far Land Kennel gave the breed Ch. Far Land Thundergust, thereby

A Ch. Son of Min T'sing son,
Ch. Clairedale Son Too.

Ch. Farland Thundergust,
by Ch. Clairedale Son Too.

Ch. Tally-Ho Black Image of Storm, another top winner in his time with three all-breed Bests in Show. Mrs. Bonney was the breeder of this Thunderstorm son.   *Tauskey*

The Thundergust son, Ch. Farland Thunderstorm, who became a big winner and important sire for Mrs. L. Bonney, Tally-Ho Kennels.

Miss Kathleen Staples bred to Black Image of Storm and produced yet another winner in Ch. Jimmee Boy.

enabling Tally-Ho Kennels to have success with Ch. Far Land Thunderstorm and his son Ch. Tally-Ho Black Image of Storm. A partner to Mrs. Bonney, Kathleen Staples, bred and owned the Black Image of Storm son, Ch. Jimmee Boy.

Additional, active exhibitors during the thirties included: Mrs. A. V. Hallowell, Lle Wol Lah; Mr. and Mrs. Barney J. Houston, Shang-Hi; Katherine Kandra, Wyndcrest; Mrs. Waldo Marra, De Lamar; Mrs. William L. Fitzgerald, Oolong and Livingston B. Osborne.

From a series of informative articles included within the Chow Chow Club's 1932 Show Catalogue and Year Book came one entitled "Chows of 1919-1931" written by Mrs. William S. Baer of Moosilauke Kennels fame. She presented statistics showing the American-bred dogs beginning to have an edge over their English-bred cousins in class wins. The English-bred Chows taking all-breed Best in Show wins were: James C. Baker's Ch. Victorious of Tien H'sia, Mr. William Crawford's Ch. Nee Phos of Manchoover and Mrs. Earl Hoover's Ch. Choonam Brilliantine of Manchoover. The American-bred dogs taking all-breed Bests included: John Z. Adams' Ch. Lord Cholmondeley, Mrs. Penney's Ch. Son of Min T'sing and the top winner, Mrs. Seamer's Ch. Yang Fu Tang.

Ch. Yang Fu Tang was bred by Richard Hoffman, Yang Fu Kennels, and was sold to Louise Seamer to be campaigned. Campaigned he was, to the extent that he set a long held record of twenty-two all-breed Bests in Show. It wasn't seriously challenged until Ch. Ah Sid the Dilettante came along to tie the record in 1963 and shatter it with his twenty-sixth Best in Show in 1964. Buddy's accomplishment would stand until 1984 when Ch. Wah-Hu Redcloud Sugar Daddy retired after thirty-five Bests.

Interestingly, the point scale for Division No. 1—East and North (comprised of ME, NH, VT, MA, CT, RI, NY, NJ, PA, MD, DE, DC, OH, IN, IL, MI and WI) in 1932 was: for one point, four dogs were required to compete; for two points, eight dogs; for a three-point major, twelve; to make a four-pointer, seventeen and for the big five point major, twenty-four Chows were needed.

The advertised stud fees ranged from $30.00 for an "Importation at Stud" introductory fee to $100.00 for Ch. Choonam Brilliantine of Manchoover who was touted as having sired twelve champions at that time. In a later tribute to Brilliantine, Ronald Beltz wrote of that fee eventually reaching $150.00 and the American champion get totalling at least fourteen.

Eng. and Am. Ch. Choonam Brilliantine of Manchoover, who was purchased by Mrs. Earl Hoover for what would today translate to about ten thousand dollars. Fortunately, he became an important show dog and foundation sire.

Ch. Yang Fu King (Int. Ch. Choonam Brilliantine ex Victoria of Manchoover), Sire of Ch. Yang Fu Tang.

Ch. Yang Fu Tang, produced by combining the bloodlines of Brilliantine and Win Sum Min T'sing, was the breed's first major winner of Best in Show awards, with twenty-two. He died from heat prostration at age seven, but left a legacy of many champion get.

Ch. Pitchi Wu Linnchow, owned and bred by Linnchow Kennels. Sire Ch. Ming Loo Sin ex Loh Moh Linnchow. The dam of six champions, she was a combination of Clairedale, Blue Monarch, and Yang Fu Tang bloodlines.

Ch. Nee Phos of Manchoover, an English-bred Best in Show winner for his owner, Mrs. William Crawford, Wauchow Kennels.

Ch. Linnchow Chu Fu II, a group winner and top sire for the Schmidts. He sired fourteen champions, four of which were group winners and a fifth, Ch. Linnchow Li Fu, a Best in Show dog.

Ch. Linnchow Li Fu, owned and bred by the Linnchow Kennels, was the winner of many Bests of Breed, several groups and one all-breed Best in Show. His sudden death at seven years was a severe blow. Sire of six champions. His dam produced five champions and her bloodlines were a combination of Yang Fu Tang and Blue Monarch breeding.

Ch. Fluji Linnchow, owned and bred by Linnchow Kennels, won several Bests of Breed and was also a group winner. Sire: Ch. Linnchow Ho Chow ex Nu Nui Linnchow, C.D.—a combination of Clairedale and Blue Monarch breeding.

During the thirties, notable personalities on the East Coast included: Mrs. Frederick Humpage with her Dingley Dell and Pagemoor Chows; Lola Thompson (eventually Bibber); Hugo and Anny Prinz, El-Cher Kennels; Eva Chase, Ho-Han Chows; Roland L. Smith, known for his multi-Specialty winner Ch. Wu Chang Tu and Robert E. Smith, a breeder-judge columnist.

The Illinois region was dominated by the Linnchow Kennels of the H. P. Schmidts during the thirties and forties. The Schmidts' daughter, Dr. JoAnne O'Brien, continues to use the registered Linnchow name today. The best known of their dogs were: Ch. Linnchow Chu Fu II, called Champie, who was a multi-group winner and the sire of sixteen champions; his half-sister, Ch. Fluji Linnchow and his son, Ch. Linnchow Li Fu who joined with Champie in retiring a Parent Club Challenge Trophy. JoAnne fondly recalls Ch. Pitchi Wu Linnchow as having been one of the family's best brood bitches.

George and Nina Armitage were active in showing, breeding and serving the Parent Club. Their Ge-Ni Chows were often winners at the New England shows. However, the couple's promising involvement with the breed was tragically ended. Unlike today, when we will hear an announcer say ". . . pending notification of next of kin" when names of accident victims are withheld, Nina wasn't privately notified. Instead, as she lay in traction with a broken back in the hospital, she heard over the radio that George's private plane had crashed over the Allegheny Mountains. All aboard were killed: George; his handler Frank Fletcher; Frank's wife and year-old child; the Chow Chow Club president Mrs. Preston; the CCC secretary, Mrs. Maxson and her husband, Dr. Maxson and several Chows. The group had been headed for the St. Louis Specialties. Nina eventually weathered that disaster and went on to serve as the CCC secretary-treasurer until her own death.

Mex. Am. Ch. Starcrest Spy of Poppyland, Top Ten winner and one of the breed's all-time Top Producers. Owners, Pete and Howard Kendall. *Clif*

3

The Modern Chow Chow in America

MANY OF THE kennels mentioned in the previous chapter proved to have true staying power and continued into the forties and beyond. A couple who followed that sort of commitment have been Raymond and Valetta Gotschall. First starting to show in the forties, the Gotschall Kennels have finished almost forty Chows to date. The war years caused others to call it quits.

Pete and Howard Kendall's Poppyland Chows have spanned decades. They were famous for both their show careers and as foundation stock for other kennels, particularly those on the West Coast. Ch. Starcrest Spy of Poppyland and Poppyland Choo Choo are among the breed's all-time Top Producers. Spy was Best of Breed at the 1962 and 1964 Nationals and Ch. Blue Blazes of Poppyland was a Best in Show winner.

An important West Coast stud and showdog of the forties was Ch. Jo Jo Hanson, sired by Ch. West's Sun of East. Not only was Jo Jo a Best in Show winner for his owners Mr. and Mrs. Walter Hanson, but he also sired three Best in Show sons including Ch. Five Ash Jo Jo. Another star of the kennel was Ch. Hanson's Hooper Du who was breeder-owner-handled to Best of Breed at the 1949 National by Mrs. Hanson.

Ch. Jo Jo Hanson (1937-1953). By Ch. West's Son of East ex Hanson's Toujours Moi. Breeders and owners, Claire and Walter Hanson. *Ludwig*

Ch. Ghat de la Moulaine shown going Best in Show from the classes 3/27/60 under Lew Starkey. Owner Vivian Shryock handling. *Blick's*

Joining the fancy in the forties were Leroy and Georgia King and their string of Kinghai winners, notably Ch. Kinghai Jill. However, the most important contribution Georgia would make to the breed would be to introduce a medium for Chowists to advertise their own stock and to be able to locate suitable mates for their dogs. Georgia's ambition was to keep the lines of communication open among Chowists all across the country. This she originally accomplished with her magazine "The American Chow Chow." After she passed it on to someone else, she regretted her decision and longed to be an editor again. This she did in the capacity of editor for the Chow Chow Club's quarterly, formerly called "The Bulletin" and now "Chow Life." When Georgia King became a widow and Walter Hanson a widower, they married. Georgia King Hanson devoted the rest of her life to Walter and the magazine.

One couple involved in communication channels being kept open among Chowists the world over were Col. Jerry Sterling and his wife Lucille. They finished dozens of Chows under their Chang-Shi prefix, both imports and homebreds. Mr. Sterling served as president of the Parent Club for a time and Mrs. Sterling wrote a Chow column for an all-breed magazine.

Another couple to enter the Chow scene in the forties were Cliff and Vivian Shryock. Their involvement with Chows included owning and training the group-winning dog, Ch Wu-Ho, C.D., as well as promoting the French import Ch. Ghat de la Moulaine to being one of the Top Producers of all time, only to be bested by descendants of his. They imported and campaigned the most titled bitch in breed history, Eng., Am., Mex. and Can. Ch. Ukwong Fleur. Both have served as officers of the Chow Chow Club for many years and fulfill breed and obedience judging assignments the world over. The Shryock home in Southern California is a veritable museum of Chow memorabilia they have collected and/or won.

Harold and Cecil Lee, in the breed for over thirty-five years, finished many dogs with the Cheng-Lee prefix. One of their dogs, Ch. Almoh, used to hang out their sports car window for hours on end while it was parked, watching the world go by. Both of the Lees have judged the breed at various regional Specialties across the country.

Dr. Imogene P. Earle established her famous Pandee Kennel in Maryland during the forties. With her background in animal nutrition, Dr. Earle saw that her Chows were fed properly. It seemed stew pots were cooking around the clock at Pandee. The diet

Eng. Am. Mex. and Can. Ch. Ukwong Fleur winning the group in Mexico under the late Fred Young. Breeders, Joan and Eric Egerton. Owners and handlers, Clif and Vivian Shryock.

Ludwig

B.I.S. winner Ch. Pandee's Jubilee. By Mi-Pao's Sinjo x Pandee's Cin Nee Linnchow.

combined with Dr. Earle's insistence on soundness produced a hardy and winning strain. Dr. Earle's associate, Dr. JoAnne O'Brien, usually handled all the Pandee Chows to their numerous Specialty, Group and Best in Show wins. The Pandee dogs were forever retiring Specialty trophies or helping other bloodlines and kennels to do the same. Notable Best in Show Chows from Pandee included: Ch. Pandee's Jubilee, Ch. Pandee's Alpha Sing and the bitch, Ch. Pandee's Red Sing.

Hal and Marie Allen began their Tsang-Po Kennels in the forties. When ill health forced them to take it easy, their foster daughter, Patricia North and her husband, Dr. Ed North would continue to breed and show on a large scale. Several Tsang-Po bitches became Top Producers. Ch. Tsang-Po's Ming Lee still holds the breed record with sixteen AKC champions to her credit. Ming Lee's dam, Ch. Tsang-Po's Kwai Chy is rated third all-time Top Producer. The kennel produced several Best in Show dogs including the show dog and Top Producer Ch. Tsang-Po's Storm Trooper. In addition, Hal Allen was a respected judge and Dr. North served as president of the Parent Club.

Over fifty champions have carried the Charmar banner since the kennel was begun in 1939 by Charles and Marjorie Evans. Mrs. Evans relied heavily on American bloodlies and had considerable success with them. Charmar Ying Hua of Wah-Hu was the dam of Ch. Wah-Hu Redcloud Sugar Daddy who holds the record for the Chow with the most all-breed Best in Show wins.

The Luck-ee Kennels of S. E. and Grace Luckey began in the mid-forties. Of the more than twenty champions that Mrs. Luckey has owned and/or bred, her best known are Am. Can. Ch. Yangtze's Model Son and his son, Am. Can. Ch. Luck-ee Model Lao Tang, both top winners in their day.

The Glenmont Kennel of John and Agrippina Anderson was best known for the striking male Ch. Dai Fu King of Glenmont. He was a multi-Best in Show winner and a successful sire. The Pandee Chows began with a Dai Fu King son, Ch. Pandee's Pooh Bah. Mrs. Anderson was an officer of the Parent Club for many years and was held in high regard as a judge.

Bessie Van Deusen Volkstadt bred Chows for over three decades with the Nor-Ton kennel prefix. Quite a number of her Chows' names also contained the word "moon" in them. More than seventy-five champions produced at Nor-Ton and one, Ch. Nor-Ton's Kim Sing, was a Best in Show winner.

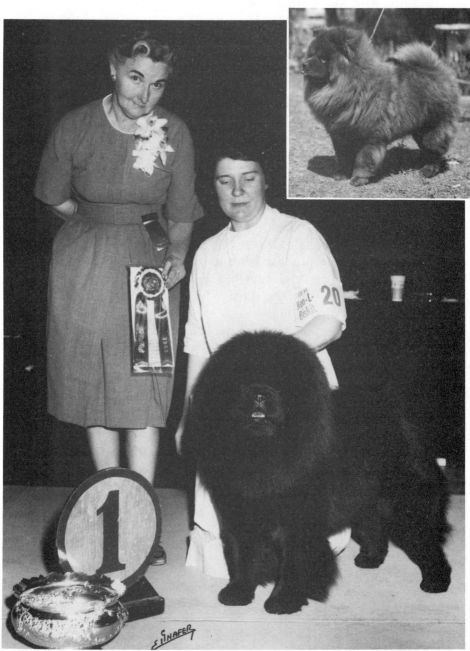

Dr. Jo Anne O'Brien handling the puppy, Pandee's Alpha Sing, to Best of Breed at the 1963 Southern CCC Specialty, under breeder-judge Florence Broadhurst. Alphie became a multi-Best in Show winner for his owner Joel Marston. Ch. Pandee's Red Sing, (inset) one of only four bitches to ever go Best in Show in America. *Lower photo E. Shafer*

Hal Allen, the founder of Tsang-Po, grooming one of his dogs.

Ch. Tsang-Po's Storm Trooper, multi-B.I.S. dog and a Top Producer. Bred by Tsang-Po and owned by Lakeview Kennels. *Graham*

Grace Luckey's Best in Show
winner Am. Can. Ch. Yangtze's
Model Son, pictured at thirteen
years of age.

Ch. Yangtze's Debutante,
a group winner in 1948.
Breeders, David and
Gladyce Kloeber and
owners, Mr. and Mrs. S.E.
Luckey.   *Jon-Syb*

Pictured in 1940, Charmar
Ching, C.D., one of Marjorie
Evans' original dogs.

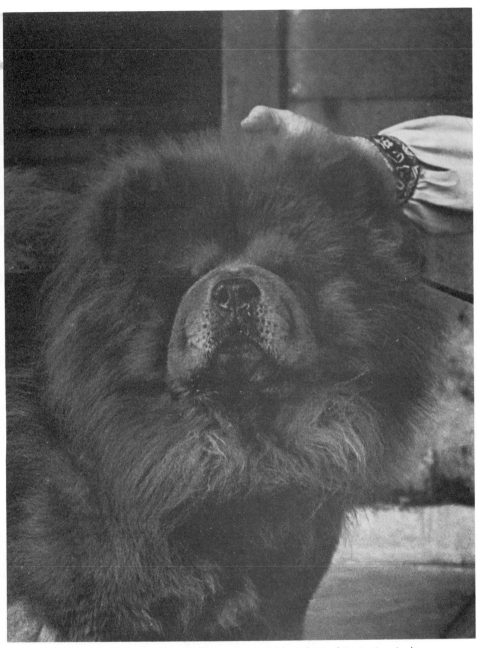

Multi-B.I.S. dog, Ch. Dai Fu King of Glenmont, owned by John and Agrippina Anderson.

E. Shafer

Abby Jan Betschowa has shown dogs with her Ah Jim prefix. Her Best in Show Ch. Ah Jim's Barbaric Emperor was one of her better known dogs, as was Ch. Ah Jim's Barbaric Knight.

As most of the aforementioned kennels continued to operate into the fifties, one woman who would outlast many in the number of continually succesful years of breeding and showing would be Florence Wilson Graham. Her more than sixty years of involvement with the breed produced such honors as Best in Show wins for Ch. Five Ash Jo Jo and Ch. Five Ash Vicki Jo. Her dogs, Ch. Five Ash Victory and Ch. Five Ash Kissin' George, won two National Specialties.

Floyd and Jeanne Messer had phenomenal success in breeding, exhibiting and wisely placing their Loy-Jean stock. Among their stars in the ring were the National Specialty winner Ch. Loy-Jean's Shoe Shine Boi. Their notable Best in Show dogs who were also that rare combination of Top Producers were Ch. Loy-Jean's China Boi and Ch. Loy-Jean's Chi Yan Kid. Ch. Loy-Jean's Beau Monty also figures prominently.

Mr. and Mrs. E. Crisp started their Cherokee Chows in the mid-fifties. Their Ch. Cherokee Nik-Nak was a Best in Show winner. Ann Crisp continues to owner-handle and judge the breed today.

Sidney Joan Wellborn and Jack Davis teamed up to establish the Ah Sid Kennels. Of the numerous champions the kennel turned out, two are especially recorded in Chow history: the National Specialty winner Ch. Ah Sid The Avant Garde and the dog who broke Ch. Yang Fu Tang's long standing Best in Show record, Ch. Ah Sid The Dilettante. In 1964 Buddy retired after winning twenty-six all-breed Bests in Show and two National Specialties. A third Ah Sid dog, Guardian Knight, was also a National Specialty winner.

Carole Whitlock had considerable success with her Car-Lee Chows. Many of her dogs have taken numerous group placements, but Ch. Lilbern's Chinese Red Robin was the top winner with three all-breed Bests in Show to his credit.

Betty-Mae's Sewards' Ky-Lin Kennel has produced over forty champions to date. One of the dogs she sold, Ch. Ky-Lin Black Power, became a Best in Show winner.

The Lakeview Kennel of Naomi Humphries Scott has produced many a Specialty, Group and Best in Show dog for more than thirty years. Beginning with Naomi owner-handling Ch. Chum Yong Fu Fun to Best in Show, her later partners David Reynolds and Don Aull piloted Ch. Lakeview's Mr. Lu-Kee to Supreme Chow, Ch.

National Specialty winner in 1955, Ch. Five Ash Victory. Breeder-owner, Florence Wilson Graham.

One of the many Loy-Jean Best in Show dogs, Ch. Loy Jean's China Boi, with seven all-breed Bests. Breeders, Mr. and Mrs. Floyd B. Messer.

Ch. Lakeview's Mr. Lu-Kee, the No. 1 Chow Chow (all systems) and No. 10 Non-Sporting Dog (Phillips System) for 1973. Bred by Manota Stertz and owned by Naomi Scott, Dave Reynolds and Don Aull.

The former record holder by virtue of twenty-six American all-breed Bests in Show, Ch. Ah Sid's The Dilettante.   *E. Shafer*

45

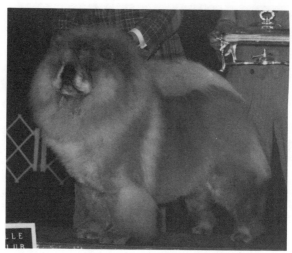

A Top Ten winner, Ch. Lakeview's Paratrooper. By Ch.
Tsang-Po's Storm Trooper x Ch. Lakeview's Holiday.

Booth

The Chow Chow Club, Inc.'s Supreme Chow for 1967, Ch. Lakeview's
Han Sum. Owner, Mamie R. Gregory.   *E. Shafer*

Tsang-Po's Storm Trooper to multiple Bests and a position of Top Producer and Ch. Lakeview's Paratrooper to some big wins. Naomi bred, but sold, Ch. Lakeview's Han Sum, who became a Supreme Chow, and his littermate, Ch. Scotchow Sum Wun, another Top Ten dog.

Joel Marston's Starcrest Chows have been the winners of everything there is to win. The dozens of Starcrest Champions have won regional Specialties and Sweepstakes from coast to coast. Ch. Starcrest Lemon Drop Kid won the National twice and his sire, Ch. Starcrest Mr. Christopher, was a Best in Show dog and a Top Producer to boot. Ch. Pandee's Alpha Sing, Ch. Starcrest Andy of Lu-Hi, Ch. Starcrest Thundergust and Ch. Starcrest Surmount figure among those capturing the top awards. Both Joel and June Marston owner-handled most of the dogs they owned, which made the wins even more commendable. Joel owns but a few Chows now and is more involved in judging than exhibiting them.

The sixties began with a French import, Ch. Ghat de la Moulaine, making Chowists across the country sit up and take notice, whether they liked him or not. The drama was basically the same as it had been in the earlier part of this century. Fanciers then had argued American-bred versus English-bred. Clif and Vivian Shryock campaigned Ghat, owner-handled, to the number one spot in 1960. He was frequently used at stud and his get began to not only finish their championship requirements, but to produce champion offspring themselves. The Ghatlings, as they were called, started filling the Top Ten spots each year, as did the next generations. Ghat's life ended tragically when he drowned in a swimming pool, but he left a legacy of being one of the all-time Top Producers of the breed and the grandsire of over two hundred American champions when the Shryocks once attempted to add them up.

In the sixties, Bob and Jean Hetherington, together with Dr. Samuel Draper, purchased a double Ghat grandson, Ch. Eastward Liontamer of Elster from the West Coast. He would soon turn the East Coast around, much as Ghat was doing in the West. Ch. Eastward Liontamer of Elster, called Louie, went on to win the National Specialty an unprecedented five times. Louie's handler, Ted Young, piloted him to many Bests in Show and the Chow placed as the #7 Chow in 1966, #2 Chow in 1967, #8 Non-Sporting Dog in 1969, #5 Non-Sporting Dog in 1970 and 1971 and #9 Chow in 1972. To join in that elite group of Chows who not only win but produce,

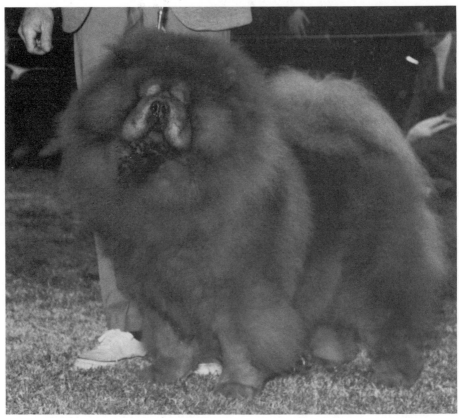

Multi-B.I.S. Ch. Starcrest Mr. Christopher, one of the breed's all-time Top Producers. Breeder-owner-handled by Joel Marston. *Ludwig*

Best in Show winner Ch. Starcrest Thundergust. Gus was
owner-handled by Larry and Nancy Ingalls.   *Kohler*

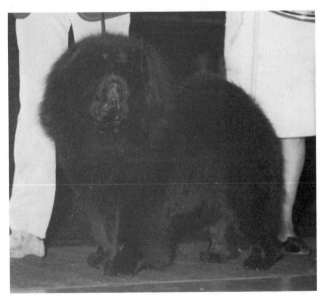

Another Mr. Christopher B.I.S. son, Ch. Starcrest Andy of
Lu-Hi. Handler, George Boulton.   *Bennett*

The CCC, Inc.'s Supreme Chow for 1975 and 1976 and B.O.B. at the National Specialty those years, Ch. Starcrest Lemon Drop Kid, with breeder-owner-handler Joel Marston.

Bergman

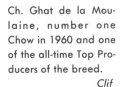

Ch. Ghat de la Mou-
laine, number one
Chow in 1960 and one
of the all-time Top Pro-
ducers of the breed.

Clif

Ch. Eastward Liontamer of Elster (1964-1975), a Ghat double grandson. "Louie" won
ten Bests in Show for his owners, Dr. Samuel Draper and Mr. and Mrs. Robert
Hetherington, Jr. *Tauskey*

Louie followed in the footsteps of his Top Producer ancestors and became one himself.

Sam Draper and his partner Desi Murphy adopted the name Liontamer for their kennel. Year after year, Desi has owner-handled Chows they have bought to multiple Bests in Show and countless group wins. They include: Ch. Ah Sid Liontamer Jamboree whose two all-breed Bests and one hundred group placements put him in the Chow Chow Club Top Ten from 1973 through 1978; Ch. Jen-Sen's China Bear of Palm, the CCC's Supreme Chow in 1982 who retired after five all-breed Bests and seventy-three group placements; Ch. Don-Lee Chowtime, in the Top Ten for four years with one all-breed Best in Show and fifty-six group placements and Ch. Foon Ying Morningstar Magic whom they are presently campaigning. Sam was the AKC delegate and an officer of the Chow Chow Club for many years and is a judge seen at shows from coast to coast.

Rick and Reba Donnelly began their Don-Lee kennel with the encouragement and breeding stock from California fanciers. Of the many Don-Lee champions, two are best remembered: the Top Ten winner Ch. Don-Lee's Chowtime and the breed's all-time Top Producer, Ch. Don-Lee's Prophet who left a legacy of sixty-two AKC champion get and countless champions in future generations.

Arthur and Ann Beamer followed strict linebreeding and inbreeding that stamped a very definite type on the Beamer Chows. One of the breed's all-time Top Producers, Ch. Beamer's Chummy Chinaman, was the sire of the #1 Top Producer, Ch. Don-Lee's Prophet and the grandsire of another Top Producer, Ch. Tsang-Po's Storm Trooper.

Audrey and Richard Meaney, Audrich, were in the fancy for a relatively short time, but the champions they produced went on to become Register of Merit and/or Top Producers for other kennels. Behind many of today's top winners you will find Ch. Audrich Star From the East, Ch. Audrich Angus Mac Tavish, Ch. Audrich Paprika of Teabear or her full sisters, Ch. Audrich Circe and Ch. Audrich Cassandra.

Harold and Adie Toudt established their Cia Hsi kennel in the late sixties and have continued to work for the breed, primarily through Adie's total involvement as the Orthopedic Foundation for Animals representative for the Chow Chow Club, Inc. They have owned and shown numerous Chow bitches to Best of Opposite Sex wins at regional Specialties across the country. They presently are

Ch. Ah Sid Liontamer Jamboree, Best in Show winner and owner-handled into the Top Ten in 1973, 1974, 1975, 1976, 1977 and 1978 by Desi Murphy for co-owner Dr. Sam Draper.

The 1982 Supreme Chow, five-time B.I.S. Ch. Jen-Sen's China Bear of Palm. Owner-handled by Desmond J. Murphy for co-owners Mae Palm and Stonybrook Kennels. *Ashbey*

B.I.S. Ch. Don-Lee Chowtime, in the Top Ten for four years. Owners Desmond Murphy, handler, and Susie Donnelly.

The top Chow Chow sire of all-time, Ch. Don-Lee's Prophet, with sixty-two AKC champion get. Breeders and owners, Rick and Reba Donnelly. *Clif*

Another Top Producer who also was the sire of Ch. Don-Lee's Prophet, Ch. Beamer's Chummy Chinaman. Breeders and owners, Art and Ann Beamer.

Ch. Audrich Paprika of Teabear, one of the Register of Merit Chows bred by Audrey and Richard Meaney. Paprika was the foundation bitch for this author.

campaigning a rarity, the B.I.S. winning bitch, Ch. Chia Hsi Go For The Gold.

Don Drennan built his successful Dre-Don kennel by combining the top bloodlines he could find. His foundation sire, Ch. Loy-Jean's Chi Yan Kid was not only in the Top Ten for three years but became one of the breed's Top Producers with his twenty-three AKC champion get. Don had Ch. Gotschall's Van Van campaigned to four all-breed Bests in Show. Don presently is meeting the challenge of working his dogs in obedience.

The Fa-Ci kennel of Jim and Betty Facciolli were active for a relatively short time before Jim's health forced them to give up the strain of showing and breeding. Their males were named after trees and their bitches after flowers. Many of these—Tamarack, Willow, Ghenko, Yucca, Black Iris, Cineraria and the Top Producer Ch. Fa-Ci Chinkapin—are to be found in the pedigrees of recent years' top winners. The Facciollis are presently involved with producing show fowl.

The Plainacre Chows of Manota Stertz partnered with Bob and Mary Wuest after Manota's ill health slowed her down. The Top Producer Plainacre's Belle Chien can be found in countless pedigrees. Plainacre's Kemo Kim sired numerous champions, notably the Top Ten winner and Top Producer Ch. Melody's Saint Noel. To sum it up, Mary explains that the Plainacre dogs have gone on to help many other kennels across the country find success.

Joan M. Hannephin began her Scotchow kennel in the mid-sixties. Of her many successful breedings to Ch. Eastward Liontamer of Elster came the stunning, group-winning bitch Ch. Scotchow Liontamer Louise. Perhaps the best known of her group winning dogs were Ch. Scotchow Sum Wun of Lakeview and Ch. Scotchow Liontamer Frankee. Many of the Scotchow champions were handled by Joan and her friend Dr. Nancy Lenfesty.

The Tamarin kennel of Prudence Baxter has seen successful in both conformation and obedience wins. Ch. Tamarin Midnight Idol was the #1 Chow in 1974. Ch. Hung Jai Lin Fa, U.D., was the first Chow ever to earn that difficult obedience degree. Pru is also active in a Chow rescue service. With the increase in unwanted or abandoned Chows, Pru and her friends try to find suitable homes to adopt the Chows. Additionally, as the smooth Chow is now written into our Standard, Pru is busy promoting it.

Jack and Dusten Cox, Dus-ten's Chows, finished many a dog

A rarity, the B.I.S.-winning bitch Ch. Chia Hsi Go For The Gold. Breeders, Harold and Adie Toudt and owners, Dean and Bev Kucker. *Phoebe*

The multi-B.I.S. Ch. Gotschall's Van Van by Ch. Loy-Jean's Chi Yan Kid x Gotschall's Dusty. Breeder, Valetta Gotschall; owner, Donald L. Drennan. *Brown*

The transformation of Manota Stertz and her Plainacre dogs. Manota with Ch. Plainacre's Tu Tang's Wun (above) in the early forties and with Ch. Plainacre's Gadabout in 1977 (below).

Another one of those rarities: a multi-group-winning bitch, Ch. Scotchow Liontamer Louise. She was handled by Dr. Nancy Lenfesty for owner Joan Hannephin. *E. Shafer*

A group winner, Ch. Scotchow Liontamer Frankee. Breeders, Sam Draper and Jean Hetherington; owner, Joan Hannephin. *Norton of Kent*

The biggest winner to come from the Pinewood Kennel, Ch. Pinewood's Renaissance, with eight Bests in Show. He was handled by Ric Byrd for breeders-owners George and Connie Boulton. *Robert*

Ch. Cheries Jubilee of Rebelrun had three B.O.S. wins at CCC, Inc. National Specialties. "Holly Berry" was the Chow bitch defeating the most Chows from 1980 through 1983.

Kohler

Ch. Imperial Allegro was breeder-owner-handled by John and Faith Reigle to the honor of being the Chow bitch defeating the most Chows in 1979.   Maurice

owner-handled. Their biggest accomplishment was making a Best in Show winner of Ch. Ky-Lin Black Power.

As the seventies approached, an influx of new faces, both canine and human, began to appear. Many came and went as never before. Perhaps it was a result of the trend to advertise more heavily than before, but people apparently couldn't cope with the dogs in the flesh as they could on paper. So, unlike dedicated Chowists of the past, many overnight breeders started to appear then disappear by the time the next magazine issue came out. Others did stay with it:

George and Connie Boulton introduced Chows to their Pinewood Kennels in the early seventies. After George's initial success in handling Ch. Starcrest Andy of Lu-Hi to an all-breed Best in Show and a Top Ten position, he and Connie went on to finish twenty-seven champions, twenty-one of which were homebreds. Of these dogs, two went on to become Best in Show winners: Ch. Pinewood's Doctor Do-Lots and Am. Can. Bda. Ch. Pinewood's Renaissance, called Rex. Rex, in the Top Ten for five years, had eight Bests in Show, 135 group placements, 8 regional Specialties and the 1983 National to his credit. A number of Pinewood Chows have finished for Register of Merit titles.

Bob and Love (Linda) Banghart have many facets to their involvement in Chows. If they're not out owner-handling their Rebelrun dogs, they are helping to hold regional Specialty shows or they can be found serving the Parent Club in a multitude of duties. Many of the Bangharts' dogs have qualified for Register of Merit titles, but their Ch. Jonel's Track Mac Tavish also went on to be an all-time Top Producer. Mac was that rare combination of being a good stud dog and doing well in the ring, as he wound up in the Top Ten for two years. One of Bob and Love's biggest winning streaks was with Ch. Cherie's Jubilee of Rebelrun, called Holly Berry. With numerous Best of Opposite Sex wins at regional and National Specialties from coast to coast, Holly Berry was the Chow bitch defeating the Chow Chows in 1980, 1981, 1982 and 1983.

Another couple who work hard for the Parent Club are John and Faith Reigle of Imperial Chows. They have owner-handled several homebreds and outside dogs to their championships. Their Ch. Imperial Allegro was the Chow bitch defeating the most Chows in 1979. Recently, their Ch. Marian's Imperial Pandy Bear has garnered Specialty and group wins and also qualified for R.O.M.

The Teabear Chows of Kip Kopatch have done their fair share of winning and producing. Of the fourteen dogs to finish their titles,

The multi-B.I.S. and nine-time Specialty B.O.B. winner Ch. Teabear's Cheese Whizz. Whizz was in the Top Ten in 1981 and 1982. He is by Ch. Pandee's Blu Cheese, ROM x Ch. Audrich Paprika of Teabear, ROM.
Gilbert

Ch. Wah-Hu Redcloud Sugar Daddy has established the present-day American all-breed Best in Show record of thirty-five. He was handled by Bill Trainor and assistant for owners Mary Vaudo and Zola Coogan.

Ch. Chinabear Gold Bullion, breeder-owner-handled by Carmen Blankenship to Best in Show. *Carol*

B.I.S. winner Ch. Chinabear Jubilation by Ch. Cabaret King of Hearts x Ch. Cheries Firewind Fiesta. Breeders, Gary and Carmen Blankenship and owners, Tom Torres and Mark Hatch. *W. Cott*

ten have been homebreds. Four Chows have gone on to qualify as R.O.M. sires and dams. The best known dog has been Ch. Teabear's Cheese Whizz who accumulated two all-breed Bests in Show, eight regional Specialties and the 1981 National. Whizz was breeder-owner-handled into the Top Ten in 1981 and 1982. Kip has also been busy with her artwork, which has been used to provide Specialty trophies, to design club, kennel and show logos and to illustrate "Chow Life" for many years.

The Cassanova Kennel was named after Robert and Judy Loratto's first winner, Ch. Pandee's Cassanova. Since that time, they have produced and/or shown dozens of champions in all colors. The highlight of their career was in 1984 when Judy breeder-owner-handled Ch. Cassanova's Isabelle to Best of Breed at the National. Only once before had it been won by a bitch. Isabelle went on to win the honor of being the Chow bitch defeating the most Chow Chows that year.

Zola Coogan of Redcloud and Mary Ann Chambers of Wah-Hu are mentioned together as a number of dogs have been exchanged between the two kennels. With dozens of rough-coated champions finished, the two women have set their sights on promoting the smooth-coated variety. Obedience training is also an interest to them. They are best recognized as Mary Ann having been the breeder of and Zola one of the co-owners of Ch. Wah-Hu Redcloud Sugar Daddy, called Billy. Billy topped the Dilettante's long-standing record of twenty-six Bests in Show by winning his thirty-fifth in 1984. He was in the Top ten for three years, being the Supreme Chow Chow in 1983 and 1984.

The Chinabear Chows of Carmen and Gary Blankenship have made their mark at the regional and national Specialties year after year. Besiders producing a number of owner-handled champions Carmen breeder-owner-handled Ch. Chinabear Gold Bullion to an all-breed Best in Show in 1987. Gary had handled Bully to Best of Breed at the National the previous year. Several of the Chinabear dogs have qualified for Register of Merit. Both Carmen and Gary have served as officers of the Parent Club.

Rob and Merideth Maddux, Sylvan Chows, have finished a number of youngsters. Their first big winner came when Ch. Redcloud Sylvan Sky Walker made it into the Top Ten in 1985 and 1986.

Gloria Plunkett, Pei-Gan Chows, is remembered for having Ch. Bu Dynasty's The Stylist campaigned into the Top Ten in 1979,

1980 and 1981, the year he was Supreme Chow. Gloria is the breeder of another Top Ten winner, Ch. Pei-Gan Maxim of Redcloud.

Ch. Pei-Gan Maxim of Redcloud was a Top Ten winner for Karen Abbott Henderson. She has owner-handled Max to the Best in Show spot in 1987. Karen has also finished quite a few homebreds under her Baybeary kennel name.

Cherie's Chow Chows are owned by Sherrie Harper and partner Jan Montayne. Their cinnamon bitch, Ch. Cherie's Chablis O'Prophet was an all-time Top Producer. Chablis had the added distinction of being the dam of the Supreme Chow Ch. Cherie's Prince Kim Hi O'Jody and of the Chow bitch defeating the most Chows for four years in a row, Ch. Cherie's Jubilee of Rebelrun. Several of Cherie's Chows have qualified for R.O.M. including Ch. Cherie's Hannibal of St. Noel.

Speaking of Saint Noel, the Checkmate Kennel of Dan and Kim O'Donnell comes to mind. The couple owned and campaigned Ch. Melody's Saint Noel to multiple Bests in Show, Best of Breed at the 1978 National and Top Ten placements. Used extensively at stud, Yon sired 50 AKC champions, including Top Ten winner Ch. Checkmate's Indiana Jones, to earn himself the honor of being one of the breed's all-time Top Producers. Two of his daughters became Top Producers also.

The Claymont Kennel of Richard, Kellie and Jo Anne Jaggie boasts top awards on several of their Chows. The aforementioned Top Producer, Claymont Lin Chu of Checkmate, was owned by them. Jo Anne owner-handled her bitch Ch. Claymont's Litany to an all-breed Best in Show and numerous group placements. Only three other bitches in the history of the breed had ever accomplished this in America. Kellie and Jo Anne owner-handled Ch. Claymont's New Edition of Noel to multiple all-breed Bests, the 1985 National and a Top Ten spot for 1984, 1985, 1986 and 1987. Jo Anne also judges Chows at Specialties across the country.

The Cabaret Chows of Joan and Jim Richard were blessed with a Top Producer, Ch. Audrich Star From The East, as their foundation bitch. Their daughter Jamie handled Ch. Cabaret Joker to two of his six all-breed Bests in Show when she was only sixteen years old. Joker was a Top Ten winner. The Richards produced Ch. Cabaret Candy Man, who, besides being an all-time Top Producer, was the sire of the breed's all-time top winner, Sugar Daddy. Of the

The multi-B.I.S. and B.I.S.S. Ch. Cherie's Prince Kim Hi O'Jody, a son of a multi-B.I.S. and multi-Specialty B.O.B. dog Ch. Starcrest Lemon Drop Kid x Ch. Cherie's Chablis O' Prophet. Breeder, Sherrie Harper; owners, Beryl and Alfred Wical.

Am. Mex. Ch. Cherie's Hannibal of St. Noel completed his Mexican title breeder-owner-handled by Sherrie Harper. He is by Ch. Melody's Saint Noel x Ch. Cherie's Chablis O' Prophet.   *Ludwig*

69

One of the breed's all-time Top Producers, Ch. Melody's Saint Noel, sire of fifty champio
Owner-handled by Dan O'Donnell for co-owner Kim O'Donnell.   *Lango*

Claymont Lin Chu of Checkmate became one of the Top Producers in the breed. She was by Ch. Tsang-Po's Bamboo Boy x Plainacres Charman Freebee.

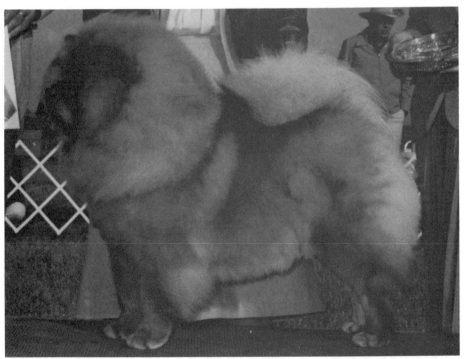

Ch. Claymont's Litany, one of only four bitches ever to take an American Best in Show. She was breeder-owner-handled by Jo Anne Jaggie to the B.I.S. win under judge Frank Haze Burch.

Ritter

Ch. Sweetkins King Crab was breeder-owner-handled by Art Friedman. Hoover is by Ch. Sweetkins of Albelarm x Ch. Sweetkins Maxine of Koby. He later became the #1 dog, all breeds, in Japan. *Klein*

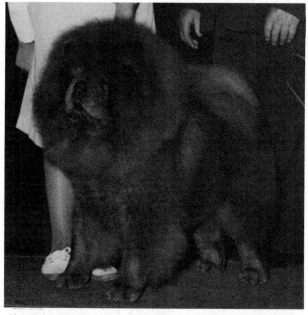

Ch. Cabaret Joker won five all-breed Bests in Show twice handled by sixteen-year-old Jamie Richard. Joker is sired by Ch. Fa-Ci Chinkapin x Ch. Audrich Star from the East, ROM.

M. Booth

many other champions the kennel has produced, one holds a conformation and obedience title, Ch. Cabaret Cracker Jack, C.D.

Michael Wolf's Mike-Mar Kennel has housed many different breeds at one time or another, and Michael has invariably had success with each one. The Chows have always appealed to him. Recently he re-entered the Chow scene and quickly made four Top Ten dogs: Ch. Koby Cassanova of Sweetkins, Ch. Sweetkins of Albelarm, Ch. Mike-Mar's Big Splash and Ch. Taichung Justin of Mike-Mar. The first three he co-owned with Mrs. A. Robson and the fourth, Justin, he bred and sold to Laura Perkinson.

Art Friedman's Sweetkins Kennel has helped launch several group-winning and all-breed Best in Show dogs. He was the breeder of Ch. Sweetkins of Albelarm, a Top Ten winner in 1981. After he finished Ch. Sweetkins King Crab and moderately specialed him here, Art sold the dog, called Hoover, to Japan where he became the #1 Dog, All Breeds in 1986.

Kathy Porter's Charkay Kennel produced many Specialty winners and two Top Ten dogs: Ch. Charkay's Lord Calvert O'Palm and the multiple Best in Show dog, Ch. Charkay's Grand Marnier O'Palm. With her marriage to George Beliew, Imagine Chows, they have bred and campaigned Ch. Imagine Calvin Cooler to Best in Show honors and a Top Ten spot in 1987. George and Kathy are also geared toward promoting smooth Chows to the fancy.

Mae Palm of Palm's Chows has been instrumental in helping others succeed. She was the co-breeder of Ch. Charkay's Grand Marnier O'Palm who was in the Top Ten from 1981 through 1984. She was the co-owner of the multiple Best in Show and Supreme Chow for 1982, Ch. Jen Sen's China Bear Of Palm.

Armont and Dorothy Willardsen's Sundance Chows have done some major winning at regional and national Specialties on a consistent basis. Their dogs have retired some challenge trophies in doing so and their Ch. Sundance Captain Ku-Ko EHR was a Top Ten winner.

Laura Perkinson of Taichung Chows is best known for her Ch. Taichung Justin of Mike Mar, a multiple Best in Show dog, R.O.M. sire, and a Top Ten placer in 1984, 1985 and 1986.

One of the most prolific kennels of consistently good dogs is Koby, which belongs to Steve and Wendy Kobrzycki. They breeder-owner-handle most of their Chows to their championships and encourage people to whom they sell future champions to do the same. Well-groomed and trained Chows are their hallmark. In their

Multi-B.I.S. and Specialty B.O.B. winner Ch. Charkay's Grand Marnier O' Palm received his first B.I.S. breeder-owner-handled by Kathy Porter. Co-breeder was Mae Palm. By Lord Calvert bred back to his dam.   *Meyer*

Ch. Charkay's Lord Calvert O' Palm was breeder-owner-handled by Kathy Porter to multiple group wins while still a puppy. By Ch. Sharbo The Demon x Ch. Charkays Creme Chablis O' Palm.

M. Booth

74

B.I.S. Ch. Imagine Calvin Cooler by Ch. Wah-Hu Charkay's Beaujolais x Pandee's Myra. Breeders and owners, George and Kathy Beliew.

Missy

Two smooth Chows, Imagine Tamarin Gold Velvet and her daughter, Imagine Tangueray N Tonic.

Multi-B.I.S. winner and Top Ten placer, Ch. Koby Cassanova of Sweetkins. Breeders, Steve and Wendy Kobrzycki; owners, Mrs. Alan Robson and Michael Wolf and handler, Bobby Barlow. Sired by Ch. T'Sang Po's Storm Trooper x Ch. Plainacre's Wen Su of Kobys.

Ashbey

The 1985 CCC, Inc. National Specialty Brood Bitch class win. (Left to right) Norma Hamaker and Am. Can. Ch. Kobys Oh Jeepers, Carol Wolfmeier and Kobys Canton Cotillion, Mary Wuest and Ch. Kobys Funny Girl of Plainacres, Tom McKean and Ch. Kobys Miss Tiffany of Tori, Steve Kobrzycki and Am. Can. Ch. Kobys Smudgy Son, judge Joseph E. Gregory and Wendy Kobrzycki with the winner, Am. Can. Ch. Plainacres Wen Su of Kobys.

Valadez

Susan Cline handled Ch. Sunswept Tonka into the Top Ten in 1978, 1979, 1980 and 1981 for breeder-owner Barbara Durst. Tonka, himself a Top Producer, is the son of an all-time Top Producer, Ch. Masterpiece Chatelaine.

first seven years in the breed, Steve and Wendy produced twenty-six homebred champions. Fourteen were out of Am. Can. Ch. Plainacre's Wensu of Kobys, an all-time Top Producer who qualified for a Silver Certificate as a Producer of Distinction. Two important sons of Wen-Su's were Am. Can. Ch. Kobys Smudgy Son and the multi-Best in Show winner, Ch. Koby Cassanova of Sweetkins. Several more of their Chows are qualified to receive R.O.M. titles.

Ron and Donna Ewing owned Rodon Kennels. Ron was the breeder-owner of the Top Ten dog, Ch. Rodon's Mr. Chips and the co-owner of the multi-Best in Show youngster, Ch. Rodon's Buddy X Lin Su, whose tragic early death ended his flying career.

Barbara Durst's many Sunswept champions have qualified her for Breeder of the Year honors and qualified her sires and dams for R.O.M. titles. One, Ch. Masterpiece Chatelaine, is an all-time Top Producer. Barbara's Ch. Sunswept Tonka was in the Top Ten in 1978, 1979, 1980 and 1981.

Carol and Ron Patterson, Caron, have shown several of their Chows to regional Specialty Bests of Breed. Their most important stud has been the cinnamon Ch. Caron's Fascinatin' Rhythm who sired two Best in Show sons. One of them, Ch. Beowulf's Sherman Tangk, was handled by Carol into a 1979 Top Ten position.

Luis and Jamie Lopez, Goodtyme Chows, bred Ch. Goodtyme's José O'Shea for Jim and Vicki Osborn to campaign into a 1984 Top Ten spot.

Charles and Linda Hughes, Charlin Chows, had particular success with their Specialty and group winner, Ch. Pinewood's I Am The Boss, and the 1983 Top Ten placer, Ch. Pinewood's Pharoah of Venus, whom they owned with Cody Milligan.

As the seventies were winding down, the popularity of the Chow Chow was on the rise. In 1979, Chows were in the 26th position of popularity among the then 124 different breeds recognized by the American Kennel Club. There were 5,014 litters and 11,739 individual Chows registered with the AKC that year.

As the eighties progressed, the breed regressed in proportionate quality to the vast quantities being produced. The following chart traces this unfortunate trend:

The cinnamon sire of two Best in Show sons, Ch. Caron's Fascinatin' Rhythm. By Tsang-Po's Gunsmoke x Ch. Don Lee's Peppermint Patty. Breeders-owners, Carol and Ron Patterson.

With almost twenty American all-breed Bests in Show to his credit, Ch. Ricksha-Epic Billy B was the Top Chow for 1986 and 1987. He is by Dragonwyck Moody Blue x Ch. Robinhill Rose of Woodside. Bred by Ken Dunsire and Carol Wolfmeier and owned by W.E. Bill Burrows. His handler is Thomas A. Glassford. *Alverson*

Year	Chow Chow Ranking	Litters	Individual Dog Reg.
1979	26th	5,014	11,739
1980	24th	6,154	14,589
1981	17th	7,855	18,511
1982	13th	9,423	22,623
1983	12th	11,398	27,815
1984	11th	14,074	32,777
1985	8th	16,989	39,167
1986	6th	19,094	43,026

The early figures for 1987 show the registrations are continuing to climb. It is a rule of thumb that any breed which finds itself in the Top Twenty is in danger. Those in the Top Ten are doomed. Just as happened earlier in this century, the Chow has fallen prey to those fly-by-nighters who cause serious damage to the breed by concerning themselves only with profit. When these unscrupulous breeders face a saturated market in which they can no longer unload puppies, they exit, leaving a trail of health and temperament problems behind.

Already the overabundance of Chows has caused the breed to be targeted by veterinarians as being one of the most ill-tempered to appear in their hospitals. These misfits of dogdom are not representative of what a stable, well-socialized Chow should be.

When this author joined the fancy, the Chow Chow was in a comfortable, to her way of thinking, position of number forty-eight in popularity. This made the breed not so rare as to be unobtainable, yet Chows were saleable to those who really were interested in the breed's welfare. When the big crash does come, hopefully soon, it will at least serve to rid the breed of the profiteers. The true Chowists will then have to work extra hard to convince the public of what a truly great breed the Chow Chow is, yet not a dog for just everyone.

So, amidst the eighties' doom and gloom, we find some hope of dedication. Ken and Joan Dunsire have kept a relatively-small Robinhill Kennel. Still, their limited breedings have produced quite a number of owner-handled champions and qualified Register of Merit Chows along the way. Joan was the editor of "Chow Life" for a while. Ken, together with Carol Wolfmeier, Ricksha Chows, bred the Top Chow for 1986 and 1987, Ch. Ricksha-Epic Billy B.

Ruth Little, Nan-Li, bred Ch. Pete's Dragon of Nan-Li who was twice in the Top Ten. There are success stories for Mary and Bill Devitt, Daystar, and Mike and Ruth Kepner, Sunny Oak. The

The Chow bitch defeating the most Chows in 1985 was Ch. Delta Dawn of Kamara. She was owner-handled by Luis and Geri De Sousa. *Ashbey II*

The first smooth Chow to complete an American championship, Ch. Bearkat Little Big Man was shown by his owner-handler, Larry Pilgrim. *E. Graham*

Tamarin Red Velvet Foon Ying picked up a five-point major owner-handled by Betsy Profancik for co-owner Larry Profancik. By Tamarin Mahogany x Ukwong Velvet Touch, bred by Pru Baxter. *Booth*

Ch. Griffchow's Mar Ja's Shou Ling, owned by James and Mary Ann Griffith and handled by Houston Clark to eight Bests in Show, was the #1 Chow in 1977. *E. Graham*

Devitts bred and the Kepners owned Ch. Daystar Orion of Sunny Oak, a Top Ten winner in 1984 and the #1 Chow in 1985. Another Top Ten winner, Ch. Metz's Lemon, was breeder-owner-handled by James R. Metzler.

The following kennels have had initial successes in recent years in finishing dogs, taking Specialty wins, qualifying R.O.M. stock, and other activities conducive to dedication in the breed: E-Lin, Elaine and Linda Albert; Tai Yang, Janet Allen and Robert Jacobsen; Willogin, Bill and Ginny Atkinson; Chowlamar, Roy and Judy Bailey; Bai-Lee's, Doug and Pamela Bailey; Mi-She, Mike and Sheri Beasley; Barbary's, Barbara Becker; Biddles, Sharon Biddle; Bondsai, Dennis and Jennifer Bond; Kamara, Carl and Marcia Boudreau; V.I.P., Bambi Brackeen; Sher-Ron, the Ronald Browns; Brylea, G. Lee and Lydia Bryant; Kathleen M. Bryant; Robloi, the Burks; Kaulee, Reg., Lindy Calles and Patsy Crabtree; Moonshine, Christine Cameron; Domino, Irene and Alex Cartabio; Wotan, Peggy Casselberry; Chan, Sheree Chan; Clarcastle, Charles and Patricia Clark; Meadows, Kaye Cooper; Antigo, Fred Johnson and Janet Coopersmith; Tu-Ka's, Kathleen and Kolleen Cosby; Leatherwood, Mike and Karen Cox; Sal Mae, Lewis and Nancy Cuccia; Bear Ritz, Dr. J. Albert and Barbara DeBlois; Gemini, Carol and Edward Daley; Kiebler, Paul Davis and Bill Smith; Solemar, Geri and Louis De Sousa; Paralon, Ron and Pat Dukes; Dychow, Charles Dye; Jade West, Bob and Alberta Edmonson; Wagamuffin, Ernie and Mary Lou Engberg; Elkomac, Rita Enright and Sampan, Jackie Fertig.

More kennels one may see winning nowadays are: Pendleton, Doug and Pat Foose; Dav-Lyn, David Ford; Somerset, Bernard and Patricia Frost; Shawnee, Joseph Galbo; Redwood, John and Darlene Gentry; Bearden, Harry and Lucille Gibney; Jes-Don, Jessee Gloria; Five Grand, Betty Goodyear; Hel-Lo, Helga Gracher; Tse-Ho, Georgene Greer; Pyramid, Joseph and Carol Guarneri; Janora, Norma Hamaker; Lohan, Leonard Hanson; Canton, Lenora Harris; Sonlit, Michael and Carol Hawke; J'Hay, Joyce Hay; Windy Hills, Robert and Bernice Hendrix; B and B, Bernardine Hills; Camaron, Paula Holbrook; My-Sam, Frank and Sandra Holloway; Moonwynd, Sonny and Beth Hubbard; Mister Bear, Mary Ann Jenkins; Jung, Sylvia Jung; Harmony, Lorraine Kazlauskas; Sunburst, Harvey and Penny Kent; Ky-Le, Ernie and Joy Kitely; Milu, Michele and Lewis Klein; Nether-Lair, Janna and Bill Kohler; Helenas, Dr. Milan and Helen Kovar; Confucius, Beverly and Dean Kucker; Cha-Ow, Cindy and Dean Kurrus; Kutchina, Barbi Kutilek; La Four, Edwin and Marie LaFour; Maneland, J. L. Lander; Lan-Chu, Del Rae Lanser; Dragonwyck, Kay McIntyre; Tori, Thomas and Darlene McKean; Shomei, Dr. Beryl and Shirley McKinnerney; Melody, Judy Tarpley Madaris; Waymar, Wayne Martin; Chen Chu, Peter and Fran Martinez; North Haven, John A. Martinez; Machow, Dovie Mayes; Jubilee, Roger and Judy Mikles; Los Cerros, Cody and Myrna Milligan; Coronet, Steve and Linda Mills; Roddie's, Faye Mitchell; Jasmin, Jeff and Andrea Moore; Eastward, Merilyn Morgan; Go-Sing, Frances Ward Nahrgang; Dan-Te, Danny and Teresa Needham; Lor-Dor, Lorence and Dorothy Nipple and Haleakala, Ann Nowicki,

More present-day fanciers include: Taygram's, Patricia Oblinger; Bellyacres, Edgar and Kaye Ohlendorf; Chamisa, James Osborn; Tai Haven, Lloyd and Charlotte Palmer; Sa-Mi, Sara Parrish; Chowhaven, William and Thelma Patrick; Mai Kai, Kim Petrunia; Bearkat, Larry Pilgrim; Foon Ying, Larry and Betsey Profancik; Wyndy Acres, Ellen Quillin; Sugar Haven, Corinne and Bruce Rathbun; Ral-Lin, Linda Reed; Tejas, Greta Faye and William Reeves; Regal, Suzanne Reid; Choi Oi, Gary and Cheryl Renton; Eden, Gail Reidell; Ki Do, Dorothy Rittenhouse; Silver Creek, Jannet Robison; Keystone, Vicki Rodenberg; Chow Lair, Nancy Roeber; El Dorado, Ruth Rohrbach; Royale, Ray Roy; Mang-Ti, Donna Roy and Wizard, Charlotte Ruskin.

More kennels that will hopefully help to shape the future: Wu-Li-Pu, Barbara Samoore; Betmar, Betty Schellenberg; Shantung, Frances Schilling; Larka, Kathleen Schwenk; Paramount, Jeff and Susie Sedillos; Fu San, Ernest Shook; Ahso Fan-C, Marilyn Short; Gys'n'Dolls, Charlene Smith; Don-Ray, Reg., Bertha Smith; Daroque, Darla Smith; Sunstar, Sally Jean Smith; Mok-Tow, Tom and Liz Smith; Shoh-Dee, Diana Smothers; Kanchou, Deborah Snapp; Camelot, Arlene and Jose Solis; K-Wala-T, Marlin and Penny Spencer; Al De Bear, Alan and Delores Stamm; Smokerise, Thomas and Brenda Stanford; Sing-Fu, Scott and Sheldon Steckley; Cierra, Linda Steinsdorfer; Pepperland, Jill and Woodrow Stillwell; Suzkanuk, Cecelia Strickland; Emperor, Mary Stuller; Brigadoon, Steve and Milli Sudduth; Odyssey, Annette and Stanley Swank; Bob-Lee, the Robert Sweimlers and Gem-Star, Gene and Mary Szcepinski.

Some additional, presently-active Chowists are: Jen-Lu, Reg., Edward and Jenne Thackeray; Jujube, Katherine Thomas; Laral,

Larry and Alice Thompson; Tonopah, Rodney Torry; Dandylion, Virginia Treider; Pa-Kum, Elizabeth Turner; Anue, Judith Underwood; Hsi So, Sandra Voina; Lud Lo, Edward and Frances Weber; Hyjinx, Ann Weremlewski; Westchow, Emma West; Akai, Charlene Wichman; Boblu, Louan Wigton; Janvan, Dr. W. Van and Janet Willis; Telstar, Katherine Wilm; Windbar, Barbara Wint; Trails End, Bill Womack; Stoney Acres, Carolyn Yaratch; Gem-Mar, Jean Yetsky and Pine Acres, Bonnie and Harold Young.

The Eighties Top Ten Chows

The seventies ended with Can. Am. Ch. Mi Tu's Han Su Shang crossing the Canadian border into the States enough times to become the Supreme Chow for his owners, Herb and Joan Williams and Fred Peddie, and his breeder, Pat Robb.

The following Chows are the Top Ten for each year thereafter as ordered by the Chow Chow Club, Inc.'s statisician's committee. The #1 Chow of any given year must meet certain Parent Club requirements before it is able to be called a Supreme Chow. Therefore, the #1 Chow may not necessarily be a Supreme Chow.

According to the Chow Chow Club, Inc., the Supreme Chow must be:
1. The Chow Chow which, from November 1 through October 31, accumulates the greatest number of TOTAL DOGS DEFEATED and;
2. places Best of Breed in at least one Chow Chow Specialty Show and;
3. places Best in Show in at least one All-Breed AKC Show and;
4. is owned or co-owned by a member of The Chow Chow Club, Inc. and;
5. has OFA Certification qualified.

1980

Supreme Chow CH. CHERIE'S PRINCE KIM HI O'JOY
    Ch. Starcrest Lemon Drop Kid x Ch. Cherie's Chablis O'Prophet
    Breeder: Sherrie Harper
    Owners: L. Beryl Wical and Alfred L. Wical, M.D.
  #2 CH. RODON'S MR. CHIPS
    Rodon's Ramblin Red x Lavette
    Breeder/Owner: Ron Ewing

#3 CH. DON-LEE CHOWTIME
   Sompin of Poppyland x Ch. Tsang-Po's Daiquiri
   Breeders: Mrs. Pat North and Susie Donnelly
   Owners: Desmond J. Murphy and Susie Donnelly
#4 CH: MI-TU'S HAN SU SHANG
   Can. Am. Ch. Foo H'Sing's Mister Lin Wu x Ch. Chi-Kwang's Han
      Su-Mei
   Breeder: Pat Robb
   Owners: Herb and Joan Williams and Fred Peddie
#5 CH. BU DYNASTY THE STYLIST
   Ch. Bu Dynasty's Shang-Hi x Ch. Tao Ming's Shangri-La
   Breeders: Herb and Joan Williams and Fred Peddie
   Owners: Gloria Plunkett and Bu Dynasty Kennel
#6 CH. PETE'S DRAGON OF NAN-LI
   Ch. Audrich Tuff Stuff x Nan-Li's Licorice
   Breeder: Ruth Little
   Owners: Shirlee Twing and Teresa Schreeder
#7 CH. SUNSWEPT TONKA
   Ch. Tonto of Wu San x Ch. Masterpiece Chatelaine
   Breeder-Owner: Barbara Durst
#8 CH. PINEWOOD'S RENAISSANCE
   Ch. Starcrest Surmount x Starcrest Tigress
   Breeders-Owners: George and Claudia Boulton
#9 CH. SNOWDEN KU TI'S SHORT STUFF
   Ch. Gotschall's Chang Kou Chian x Ch. Snowden's Devlish Ku-Ti-Pi
   Breeder-Owner: Dorothy Moore
#10 CH. CHARKAY'S LORD CALVERT O'PALM
   Ch. Sharbo The Demon x Ch. Charkay's Creme-Chablis O'Palm
   Breeder-Owner: Kathy Lee Porter

1981

Supreme Chow CH. BU DYNASTY THE STYLIST
   Ch. Bu Dynasty's Shang-Hi x Ch. Tao Ming's Shangri-La
   Breeders: Herb and Joan Williams and Fred Peddie
   Owners: Gloria Plunkett and Bu Dynasty Kennels
#2 CH. PINEWOOD'S RENAISSANCE
   Ch. Starcrest Surmount x Starcrest Tigress
   Breeders-Owners: George and Claudia Boulton
#3 CH. SWEETKINS OF ALBELARM
   Ch. Checkmate's Nickelodeon x Sweetkin's China Syndrome
   Breeders: Art and Barbara Friedman
   Owners: Mrs. Alan R. Robson and Michael Wolf
#4 CH. JEN SEN'S CHINA BEAR O'PALM
   Ch. Palm's Liontamer Jack x Liontamer Fluffy of Ho-San
   Breeder: Rosalyn E. Jensen
   Owners: Mae Palm and Desmond Murphy

#5 CH. JONEL'S TRACK MACTAVISH
Jemaco Track Twenty-Nine x Jonel Angelia
Breeder: Johnie Meador
Owners: Robert and Linda Banghart

#6 CH. SUNSWEPT TONKA
Ch. Tonto of Wu San x Ch. Masterpiece Chatelaine
Breeder-Owner: Barbara Durst

#7 CH. CHARKAY'S GRAND MARNIER O'PALM
Ch. Charkay's Lord Calvert O'Palm x Ch. Charkay's Creme-Chablis
O'Palm
Breeders: Kathy Lee Porter and Mae Palm
Owners: Chuck and Kathy Lee Porter

#8 CH. TEABEAR'S CHEESE WHIZZ
Ch. Pandee's Blu Cheese x Ch. Audrich Paprika of Teabear
Breeder-Owner: L. J. Kip Kopatch

#9 CH. RHYTHM'S MAGICMAN O'STARSHINE
Ch. Melody's Rustic Rhythm x Ch. Melody's Syncopated Rhythm
Breeder: Victoria A. Helfrich
Owner: Jackie Black

#10 CH. DON-LEE CHOWTIME
Sompin of Poppyland x Ch. T'sang-Po's Daiquiri
Breeders: Pat North and Susie Donnelly
Owners: Desmond J. Murphy and Susie Donnelly

1982

Supreme Chow CH. JEN SEN'S CHINA BEAR O'PALM
Ch. Palm's Liontamer Jack x Liontamer Fluffy of Ho-San
Breeder: Rosalyn E. Jensen
Owners: Mae Palm, Desmond Murphy and Stonybrook Kennels

#2 CH. RODON'S BUDDY X LIN SU
Ch. Buddy Budweiser of Sunny Oak x Ch. Lin Su Rosie Posie of Rodon
Breeders: Ralph and Linda Carter
Owners: Ron Ewing and B. M. and S. Womack

#3 CH. PINEWOOD'S RENAISSANCE
Ch. Starcrest Surmount x Starcrest Tigress
Breeders: George and Claudia Boulton
Owner: George Boulton

#4 CH. WAH-HU REDCLOUD SUGAR DADDY
Ch. Cabaret Candy Man x Charmer Ying Hua of Wah-Hu
Breeder: Mary Ann Chambers
Owners: M. A. Vaudo and Zola Coogan

#5 CH. TEABEAR'S CHEESE WHIZZ
Ch. Pandee's Blu Cheese x Ch. Audrich Paprika of Teabear
Breeder-Owner: L. J. Kip Kopatch

#6 CH CABARET JOKER
Ch. Fa-Ci Chinkapin x Ch. Audrich Star From The East
Breeders-Owners: Joan and James Richard

#7 CH. CHARKAY'S GRAND MARNIER O'PALM
  Ch. Charkay's Lord Calvert O'Palm x Ch. Charkay's Creme-Chablis
    O'Palm
  Breeders: Kathy Lee Porter and Mae Palm
  Owners: Chuck and Kathy Lee Porter
#8 CH. KOBY CASSANOVA OF SWEETKINS
  Ch. T'sang-Po's Storm Trooper x Ch. Plainacre's Wen Su of Kobys
  Breeders: Steve and Wendy Kobrzycki
  Owners: Mrs. A. R. Robson and M. Wolf
#9 CH. STARCREST THUNDERGUST
  Ch. Starcrest Mr. Chow x Ch. Starcrest Top Cat
  Breeders: Joel and June Marston
  Owners: Larry Ingalls and Joel Marston
#10 CH. PETE'S DRAGON OF NAN-LI
  Ch. Audrich Tuff Stuff x Nan Li's Licorice
  Breeders: Wm. and N. J. Schreeder and Ruth Little
  Owners: Shirlee Twing and Ruth Little

Note: The Parent Club extended the list in 1982 to the Top Eleven as eleven
Chows had Best in Show wins and had met the minimum requirements for
Supreme Chow.

#11 CH. CLAYMONT'S LITANY
  Poggin Poy DLF x Claymont's Pun-Kin of Noel
  Breeders-Owners: Richard J. and JoAnne R. Jaggie

1983

Supreme Chow CH. WAH-HU REDCLOUD SUGAR DADDY
  Ch. Cabaret Candy Man x Charmer Ying Hua of Wah-Hu
  Breeder: Mary Ann Chambers
  Owners: M. A. Vaudo and Zola Coogan
#2 CH. PINEWOOD'S RENAISSANCE
  Ch. Starcrest Surmount x Starcrest Tigress
  Breeders: George and Claudia Boulton
  Owner: George Boulton
#3 CH. RODON'S BUDDY X LIN SU
  Ch. Buddy Budweiser of Sunny Oak x Ch. Lin Su Rosie Posie of Rodon
  Breeders: Ralph and Linda Carter
  Owners: Ron Ewing and B. M. and S. Womack
#4 CH. KOBY CASSANOVA OF SWEETKINS
  Ch. T'sang-Po's Storm Trooper x Ch. Plainacre's Wen Su of Kobys
  Breeders: Steve and Wendy Kobrzycki
  Owners: Mrs. A. R. Robson and Michael Wolf
#5 CH. CHARKAY'S GRAND MARNIER O'PALM
  Ch. Charkay's Lord Calvert O'Palm x Ch. Charkay's Creme-Chablis
    O'Palm
  Breeders: Kathy Lee Porter and Mae Palm
  Owners: Chuck and Kathy Lee Porter

#6 CH. PINEWOOD'S PHARAOH OF VENUS
Ch. Starcrest Surmount x Ch. Tsang-Po's Motsu Inu
Breeders: George and Claudia Boulton
Owners: C. Hughes and C. Milligan
#7 CH. JEN SEN'S CHINA BEAR O'PALM
Ch. Palm's Liontamer Jack x Liontamer Fluffy of Ho-San
Breeder: Rosalyn E. Jensen
Owners: Mae Palm, Desmond Murphy, and Stonybrook Kennels
#8 CH. JONEL'S TRACK MACTAVISH
Jemaco Track Twenty-Nine x Jonel Angelia
Breeder: Johnie Meador
Owners: Robert and Linda Banghart
#9 CH. LAKEVIEW'S PARATROOPER
Ch. Tsang-Po's Storm Trooper x Ch. Lakeview's Holiday
Breeders-Owners: David Reynolds, Naomi Scott and Don Aull
#10 CH. CHI DEBUT'S NUTCRACKER SUITE
Ch. Mi-Tu's Han Su Shang x Ch. Cedar Creek's Ms. Chiona Ling
Breeder-Owner: Patti Spratt

1984

Supreme Chow CH. WAH-HU REDCLOUD SUGAR DADDY
Ch. Cabaret Candy Man x Charmar Ying Hua of Wah-Hu
Breeder: Mary Ann Chambers
Owners: M. A. Vaudo and Zola Coogan
#2 CH. CHARKAY'S GRAND MARNIER O'PALM
Ch. Charkay's Lord Calvert O'Palm x Ch. Charkay's Creme-Chablis
O'Palm
Breeders: Kathy Lee Porter and Mae Palm
Owner: Kathy Lee Porter
#3 CH. KOBY CASSANOVA OF SWEETKINS
Ch. Tsang-Po's Storm Trooper x Ch. Plainacre's Wen Su of Kobys
Breeders: Steve and Wendy Kobrzycki
Owners: Mrs. Alan R. Robson, Michael Wolf and Desmond Murphy
#4 CH. PINEWOOD'S RENAISSANCE
Ch. Starcrest Surmount x Starcrest Tigress
Breeders: George and Claudia Boulton
Owner: George D. Boulton
#5 CH. TAICHUNG JUSTIN OF MIKE-MAR
Ch. Koby Cassanova of Sweetkins x Teabear's Dewberry Well
Breeder: Michael Wolf
Owner: Laura Perkinson
#6 CH. DAYSTAR ORION OF SUNNY OAK
Ch. Cannonball x Sundance Hai Li Yung Shu
Breeders: Mary and Bill Devitt
Owners: Mike and Ruth Kepner
#7 CH. JONEL'S TRACK MACTAVISH
Jemaco Track Twenty-Nine x Jonel Angelia

Breeder: Johnie Meador
Owners: Robert and Linda Banghart
#8 CH. CHECKMATE'S INDIANA JONES
Ch. Melody's Saint Noel x Ch. Checkmate's Cherry Brandy
Breeders: Dan and Kim O'Donnell
Owners: Joseph Becker and Margaret Thornton
#9 CH. CLAYMONT'S NEW EDITION OF NOEL
Ch. Melody's Saint Noel x Claymont Lin Chu of Checkmate
Breeders: Richard J. and JoAnne R. Jaggie
Owners: Kellie and JoAnne Jaggie
#10 CH. GOODTYME'S JOSE O'SHEA
Ch. Pinewood's I Am The Boss x Westchow's Miss Aster
Breeders: Luis A. and Jamie Lopez
Owners: Jim and Vicki Osborn

1985

#1 CH. DAYSTAR ORION OF SUNNY OAK
Ch. Starcrest Cannonball x Sundance Hai Li Yung Shu
Breeders: Mary and Bill Devitt
Owners: C. Anderson and Ruth Kepner
#2 CH. SUNDANCE CAPTAIN KU-KO EHR
Ch. Jemaco Capt'n Crunch x Ch. Sundance Ping Li Shu
Breeders-Owners: Armont and Dorothy Willardsen
#3 CH. REDCLOUD SYLVAN SKY WALKER
Ch. Wah-Hu Redcloud Sugar Daddy x Ch. Wah-Hu's Wing Walker
Breeder: Zola Coogan
Owner: W. Long
#4 CH. TAICHUNG JUSTIN OF MIKE-MAR
Ch. Koby Cassanova of Sweetkins x Teabear's Dewberry Well
Breeder: Michael Wolf
Owner: Laura Perkinson
#5 CH. CLAYMONT'S NEW EDITION OF NOEL
Ch. Melody's Saint Noel x Claymont Lin Chu of Checkmate
Breeders: Richard J. and JoAnne R. Jaggie
Owners: Kellie and JoAnne Jaggie
#6 CH. SONLIT IMAGINE THE DUKE
Ch. Jonel's Charlie x Sal Mae's Promise Me Roses
Breeders: George and Penny Beliew and Linda Love Banghart
Owners: Robert Banghart and Michael Hawke
#7 CH. MIKE-MAR'S BIG SPLASH
Ch. Sweetkins King Crab x Ch. Bu Dynasty B'rani
Breeder: Louise Smith
Owners: Mrs. A. Robson and Michael Wolf
#8 CH. BEAR RITZ LE GRANDE OURSE
Ch. Dav-Lyn's Lord Dunhill x Wah-Hu Redcloud Sugar Plum
Breeders: Dr. Albert J. and Barbara DeBlois
Owners: J. DeBlois and P. and V. Kimmel

#9 CH. YE BOODA'S GAN JAK JUK JINJER
Ch. Koby's Sun Yat Sen of War-Rah x Cinderella's Tara Chimo
Breeder: Paula H. Ye
Owners: Paula Ye and J. Heffington
#10 CH. RODDIE'S CLONE OF HOT SHOT
Ch. Sam-Des Hot Shot x Hungchow's Bertha
Breeders: Lynne and Lynn Campbell
Owners: Roddie and Faye Mitchell

1986

#1 CH. RICKSHA-EPIC BILLY B
Dragonwyck Moody Blue x Robinhill Rose of Woodside
Breeders: Ken Dunsire and Carol Wolfmeier
Owner: William Burrows
#2 CH. CLAYMONT'S NEW EDITION OF NOEL
Ch. Melody's Saint Noel x Claymont Lin Chu of Checkmate
Breeders: Richard J. and JoAnne R. Jaggie
Owners: Kellie and JoAnne Jaggie
#3 CH. TAICHUNG JUSTIN OF MIKE-MAR
Ch. Koby Cassanova of Sweetkins x Teabear's Dewberry Well
Breeder: Michael Wolf
Owner: Laura Perkinson
#4 CH. PEI-GAN MAXIM OF REDCLOUD
Ch. Wah-Hu Redcloud Sugar Daddy x Ralbenic Trafalger Square
Breeder: Gloria Plunkett
Owners: Karen Abbott Henderson and Zola Coogan
#5 CH. METZ'S LEMON
Bu Dynasty's Metz's Machine x Charkay's Metz's Rose
Breeder-Owner: James R. Metzler
#6 CH. YE BOODA'S GAN JAK JUK JINGER
Ch. Koby's Sun Yat Sen of War-Rah x Cinderella's Tara Chimo
Breeder: Paula H. Ye
Owners: L. Gough and Paula Ye
#7 CH. MANCHURIAN COUP DE GRACE
Ch. Chumpus Belvane Tortfeeasor x Lin Su Pebbles of Sunny Oak
Breeders: James R. and Shelle Flesland and Ruth Kepner
Owners: Ruth Kepner and James Flesland
#8 CH. CHINABEAR GOLD BULLION
Ch. Chinabear Manolete x Ch. Chinabear Golden Kamay
Breeders-Owners: Gary and Carmen Blankenship
#9 CH. RODDIE'S CROWN ROYAL RAINBOW
Ch. Goodtyme's Jose O'Shea x Campbell's Daisy Jane
Breeders: Roddie W. and Faye Mitchell and James W. and V. Osborn
Owners: Phil and Pattie Goodwin
#10 CH. REDCLOUD SYLVAN SKY WALKER
Ch. Wah-Hu Redcloud Sugar Daddy x Ch. Wah-Hu's Wing Walker
Breeder: Zola Coogan
Owners: Meredith Maddux and Zola Coogan

4

Register of Merit Sires and Dams and Top Producers

FROM WORTHY STUD DOGS and brood bitches come the winners, so, in 1986 The Chow Chow Club, Inc. began a Register of Merit (ROM) system to honor worthy sires and dams in the breed. The offspring accumulate points for their parent by way of an R.O.M., championship or obedience title, an OFA number, major and major reserve wins, Best of Breed and Best of Opposite Sex to Best of Breed wins, Group One, Best in Show and Specialty Best of Breed wins.

The dams so honored include the following: Teabear Pattycake Pattycake, owned by Ken and Joan Dunsire; Ch. Cheries Chablis O'Prophet, Sherrie Harper; Ch. Tai Yang's Tinker Toy, Janet Allen and Robert Jacobsen; Ch. Cherie's Blue Blazes of Janvan, Janet and Van Willis; Cherie's Reflections O'Chablis, Sherrie Harper; Ch. Moonwynd Dream Maker, Beth Hubbard and Jill Stillwell; Ch. Rebelrun's Scarlet Starlet, Bob and Linda Banghart; Canton Suki, Lenora Harris; Claymont Lin Chu of Checkmate, Richard and JoAnne Jaggie; Westchow's Miss Aster, Gene and Mary Szczepinski; Ch. Rebelrun's Daddy's Girl, Robert and Linda Banghart; Rebel-

Teabear Pattycake Pattycake, ROM

Ch. Robinhill Antares, ROM

Janvan Extra Special, ROM (left) with Jan Willis, her daughter Janvan Couldn't Be Cuter with Van Willis (center) and Ch. Janvan Varsity with Joan Dunsire (right). Shown winning the 1987 Golden State CCC Specialty Brood Bitch class. *Kohler*

(From left to right) Ch. Robinhill Captain Preppie, ROM, handled by Brian Greene Willis; Ch. Janvan Varsity, owner-handled by Janet Willis; Ch. Janvan Princeton of Tonopah, owner-handled by Rodney Torry and Ch. Janvan Miss Ivy League, owner-handled by Kim La Coco for co-owner Janet Willis. *Kohler*

Ch. Rebelruns Daddy's Girl, ROM

Ch. Rebelruns Scarlet Starlet, ROM

Ch. Cherie Blue Blazes of Janvan, ROM
Ludwig

Ch. Bu Dynasty The Judgement, ROM

Cherie's Reflections O' Chablis, ROM

Ch. Cherie's Chablis O' Prophet, ROM, the dam of Reflections.

Ch. Joysun Butcherblock, ROM

Ch. Cherie's Hannibal of St. Noel, ROM

Al De Bear The Velvet Touch, ROM

Ch. Moonwynd Dream Maker, ROM

Ch. Al De Bear Sox Up Starcrest, ROM

Ch. Al De Bear Hustler, ROM, sired by Ch. Al De Bear Sox Up Starcrest, ROM

Ch. Audrich Star From The East, ROM, dam of Ch. Cabaret Joker, handled by Mary Ann Whitney.

Booth

Ch. Pandee's Blu Cheese, ROM

Jemaco Teabear Bluberry Tart, ROM

Dragonwyck Moody Blue, ROM

run's Jenny Linn, Walter and Helga Balodis; Ch. Cedar Creek's Ms. Chiona Lin, John Spratt; Coronet Bisque, Steve and Linda Mills; Chinabear Strictly Tabu, Virginia Treider; Empress Chinchow Lan-Chu, Vaughn A. and Del Rae Lanser; Al De Bear The Velvet Touch, Alan and Deloris Stamm; Ch. Audrich Paprika of Teabear, L. J. Kip Kopatch; Janvan Extra Special, Dr. Van and Janet Willis; Ch. Janvan's Moonshine Cassandra, Christine Cameron; Jemaco Teabear Bluberry Tart, L. J. Kip Kopatch.

The males who have thus far qualified as R.O.M. sires include: Ch. Charlie's Hannibal of St. Noel, Sherrie Harper; Ch. Robinhill Antares, Ken and Joan Dunsire; Ch. Jonel's Track MacTavish, Bob and Linda Banghart; Ch. Al De Bear Hustler, Alan and Deloris Stamm; Ch. Melody's St. Noel, Kim O'Donnell; Ch. Silverstone's Cypress, Marjorie L. Newman; Ch. Al De Bear Pepperland Captain Midnight, Jill and Woodrow Stillwell; Ch. Joysun Butcherblock, Irene and Alex Cartabio; Ch. Taichung Justin of Mike Mar, Laura Perkinson; Ch. Bu Dynasty The Judgement, Robert and Linda Banghart; Ch. Leatherwood Matthew, Karen Cox; Ch. Robinhill Captain Preppie, Dr. Van and Janet Willis; Ch. Ghat De La Moulaine, Clif and Vivian Shyrock; Ch. Al De Bear Sox Up Starcrest, Alan and Delores Stamm; Ch. Cherie's Moonshine Sky's The Limit, Christine Cameron; Ch. Teabear's Cheese Whizz, L. J. Kip Kopatch; Dragonwyck Moody Blue, Carol Wolfmeier and Ch. Pandee's Blu Cheese, L. J. Kip Kopatch.

Top Producers

Irene Khatoonian Schlintz has kept records of the various breeds' leading sires and dams. Here are Mrs. Schlintz's rules for their qualifications and the Top Ten Producers for each sex.

"Names of prominent sires and dams will come to mind, and the reader will wonder why they are not listed in the following pages as they know they have more champion get than some whose names appear in this book. All the dogs must first qualify before a permanent record is set up.

To qualify, the sire must have had published in the "AKC Gazette, Purebred Dogs" the names of five champion offspring during a twelve month period beginning with March of one year through February of the following year. The dams have been required to have three champions of record published during the same period of time as the sires.

When I first started keeping records on top producers in 1965, practically all the results of the January shows were published in the March issue of the "Gazette" and the December shows were listed in the February issue. At the present time it takes about fifteen months to be sure all results have been printed."

Here, then, I have listed the honored Chow Chow sires and dams as established by the extraordinary Mrs. Schlintz.

A history-making bitch in the annals of breeding Chows, Pattimac Popsicle To Teabear. Her sire, Ch. Teabear's Cheese Whizz, ROM, lives in Rhode Island, but his frozen semen was shipped from a sperm bank in California to inseminate Ch. Pattimac's Lotta Love in New Jersey. The result was the first Chow to be conceived and whelped using frozen semen.   *Ashbey*

Assam de la Moulaine
Sire: Duang-Lai de la Moulaine (France)
Hang-Fung
CH. GHAT DE LA MOULAINE N507366 (2/60) Red
Ch. Ki-Dong-King
Dam: Ch. Ychouchanna V. Mongolie (France) Red
Ch. Wooley van Majodo

Ch. Ghat de la Moulaine was whelped August 31, 1957. His breeder was Rene Hassenforder of France and owners were Clif and Vivian Shryock of California. A Top Producer in 1965 and 1967, he sired the Top Producers Ch. Starcrest Spy of Poppyland, Ken-Wan's Tahg Along, Ch. Loy-Jean's Chi Yan Kid and Nor-Ton's Sparkle of Moulaine. His Top Ten get included Ch. Loy-Jean's Chi Yan Kid, the #6 Chow in 1963, #7 Chow in 1964 and #3 Chow in 1966; Ch. Starcrest Spy of Poppyland, #2 Chow in 1965 and 1966 and Ch. Loy-Jean's Beau Monty, #5 Chow in 1966. An all-breed Best in Show winner himself, Ghat was #1 Chow and #5 Non-Sporting Dog in 1960.

His thirty-six AKC champion get were out of fifteen dams. Of the fifty litters he sired, twenty were repeat breedings. Ming Wa Ti produced seven champions by him.

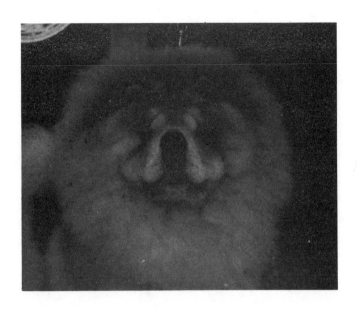

Duang-Lai de la Moulaine (France)
Sire: Ch. Ghat de la Moulaine N507366 (2/60) Red
Ch. Ychouchanna v. Mongolie (France) Red
MEX. and AM. CH. STARCREST SPY OF POPPYLAND N5903689 (9/61) Red
Ch. Chinese Heathen of Poppyland N320591 (6/58)
Red
Dam: Poppyland Choo Choo N499341 (2/60) Cream
Poppy of Poppyland N241978 (2/56) Red

Ch. Starcrest Spy of Poppyland was whelped May 10, 1960. His breeder was Joel Marston and owners were Mr. and Mrs. Howard Kendall of California. A 1965 Top Producer, Spy was by the Top Producer Ghat. Spy sired two Top Producers, Ch. Eastward Liontamer of Elster and Livin' Doll of Poppyland.

Two of Spy's get were Top Ten winners: Ch. Eastward Liontamer of Elster, #7 Chow in 1966, #2 Chow in 1967, #4 Chow in 1968, #8 Non-Sporting Dog in 1969, #5 Non-Sporting Dog in 1970 and 1971 and #9 Chow in 1972 and Ch. Kee Zee Kessaman of Cheng Lee, #9 Chow in 1970. Spy's own show record included being #2 Chow in 1965 and 1966 and #7 Chow in 1967.

Spy's fourteen AKC champion get were out of four dams, notably eight by the Top Producer Ken-Wan's Tahg Along.

Duang-Lai de la Moulaine (France)
Sire: Ch. Ghat de la Moulaine N507366 (2/60) Red
Ch. Ychouchanna v. Mongolie (France) Red
CH. LOY-JEAN'S CHI YAN KID N740599 (4/63) Red
Ch. Lu-Lon's Tass-Sir of Toi San N101527 (2/51)
Red
Dam: Ch. Loy-Jean's Princess of Hai Nan N385432 (11/59) Red
Ch. Loy-Jean's Mi Keta N127985 (3/52) Red

Ch. Loy-Jean's Chi Yan Kid was whelped August 29, 1961. His breeders were Floyd and Jean Messer and his owner Donald Drennan of New York. The son of the Top Producer Ghat, Chi Yan Kid was a 1968 Top Producer. His son, Ch. Gotschall's Van Van was the #3 Chow Chow in 1966, 1967, 1968 and 1969. Chi Yan Kid's own show career recorded him as #6 Chow in 1963, #7 Chow in 1964 and #3 Chow in 1966.

His twenty-three AKC champion get were produced by ten dams. Ch. Gotschall's Dusty provided seven champions. Four dams had one champion each.

Ch. Ghat de la Moulaine N507366 (2/60) Red
Sire: Am. Mex. Ch. Starcrest Spy of Poppyland N590368 (9/61) Red
Poppyland Choo Choo N499341 (2/60) Cream
CH. EASTWARD LIONTAMER OF ELSTER NA298752 (11/67) Red
Ch. Ghat de la Moulaine N507366 (2/60) Red
Dam: Ken-Wan's Tahg Along N649708 (7/62) Red
Fluffy Chinese Princess N330176 (10/57) Red

Ch. Eastward Liontamer of Elster was whelped November 27, 1964. His breeders were Mr. and Mrs. William Elster and owners were Bob and Jean Hetherington and Dr. Sam Draper. Louie was a 1972 Top Producer following the footsteps of his dam, Tahg Along; his sire, Spy; and his double grandsire, Ghat.

The twenty-seven AKC champions by Liontamer were out of fourteen dams. Scotchow Samantha accounted for five. Eight dams whelped one champion each. Offspring included Top Ten winners Ch. Scotchow Liontamer Louise, #8 Chow in 1968; Ch. Liontamer Mardi Gras, #7 Chow in 1969, #3 Chow in 1970, 1971 and 1972, #7 Chow in 1973 and #10 Chow in 1974; Ch. Scotchow Liontamer Frankee, #7 Chow in 1970 and #8 Chow in 1972 and Ch. Ah Sid Liontamer Jamboree, #5 Chow in 1973, #9 Chow in 1974, #7 Chow in 1975 and #4 Chow in 1976.

Ch. Eastward Liontamer of Elster was a multi-Best in Show dog and the National Specialty winner five times. He was #7 Chow in 1966, #2 Chow in 1967, #8 Non-Sporting Dog in 1969, #5 Non-Sporting Dog in 1970 and 1971 and #9 Chow in 1972.

Ch. Jean's Sammee Tong N579416 (6/62)
Sire: Beamer's Beau Chien NA145989 (12/64) Red
Macherie de la Moulaine N766378 (2/63) Red
CH. BEAMER'S CHUMMY CHINAMAN NA318919 (3/67) Red
Beamer's Willie Chum N442416 (3/60) Red
Dam: Ch. Beamer's Suzette NA145993 (4/65) Red
Macherie de la Moulaine N766378 (2/63) Red

Ch. Beamer's Chummy Chinaman was whelped October 27, 1964. His breeders and owners were Mr. and Mrs. Arthur Beamer of Ohio. A Top Producer in 1971 and 1974, Chummy was the sire of the breed's all-time Top Producer, Prophet.

Chummy sired two Top Ten winners: Ch. Plain Acre's Char Man Fella, the #9 Chow in 1968 and 1969 and Ch. Lakeview's Mr. Lu-Kee, #2 Chow in 1972 and #1 Chow in 1973.

Ch. Beamer's Chummy Chinaman was the sire of twenty-four AKC champion get out of nine dams. One of those, Plain Acre's Belle Chien, was a Top Producer herself, with nine champions.

Beamer's Beau Chien NA 145989 (12/64) Red
Sire: Ch. Beamer's Chummy Chinaman NA318919 (3/67) Red
Ch. Beamer's Suzette NA145993 (4/65) Red
CH. DON-LEE'S PROPHET NB960992 (2/72) Red
Ch. Starcrest Mr. Christopher NB272998 (7/69) Red
Dam: Ch. Don-Lee's Jewel of Ho-San NB529757 (7/70) Red
Livin' Doll of Poppyland NA819442 (1/68) Red

Ch. Don-Lee's Prophet was whelped August 8, 1970. His breeders and owners were Rick and Reba Donnelly of California. A Top Producer every year from 1974 through 1980, he was the son of a Top Producer, Chummy Chinaman. Among Prophet's get were the Top Producers Ch. Cherie's Chablis O'Prophet, Ch. Tsang-Po's Motsu Inu, Ch. Tsang-Po's Storm Trooper and El Perro Ozo's Wild Honey. He also sired a Top Ten winner, Ch. Caron's Bhutan Buddha, the #6 Chow Chow in 1976. Prophet's sixty-two AKC champions were out of twenty-six dams, eleven of which had but one champion each.

Ch. Beamer's Chummy Chinaman NA318919 (3/67)
Red
Sire: Ch. Don-Lee's Prophet NB960992 (2/72) Red
Ch. Don-Lee's Jewel of Ho-Sa NB529757 (7/70)
Red
CH. TSANG-PO'S STORM TROOPER NS267326 (6/77) Red
Ch. Shanglo's Tishmingo NA429505 (8/67) Red
Dam: Ch. Tsang-Po's Ming Lee NB362337 (9/70) Red
Ch. Tsang-Po's Kwai Chy N4962912 (8/67) Red

Ch. Tsang-Po's Storm Trooper was whelped October 16, 1975. He was bred by Tsang-Po Kennels and owned by David Reynolds, Naomi Scott and Don Aull of Kentucky. A Top Producer in 1980 and 1982, Storm Trooper was a third generation Top Producer on both sides. His sire was the all-time Top Producer Prophet and his grandsire was Chummy. His dam, Ming Lee and granddam, Kwai-Chy, were both Top Producers.

Storm Trooper sired two Top Ten winners: Ch. Koby Cassanova of Sweetkins, #7 Chow in 1982, #5 Chow in 1983 and #3 Chow in 1984 and Ch. Lakeview Paratrooper, #10 Chow in 1983.

Storm Trooper's sixteen AKC champion get were out of nine dams. Top Producer Ch. Plainacre's Wen Su of Kobys accounted for five, while six dams had but one champion each.

Ch. Pandee's Jubilee NA558428 (4/67) Red
Sire: Starcrest Jupiter of Pandee NA847693 (6/68) Cin.
Pandee's Zip Orah NA422204 (4/67) Cinnamon
CH. STARCREST MR. CHRISTOPHER NB272998 (7/69) Red
Ch. Starcrest Richard The Lion N553192 (3/61) Red
Dam: Ch. Starcrest Witch Away NA494067 (2/69) Black
Ch. Indian Star's Yu-Lui N883192 (1/65) Black

Ch. Starcrest Mr. Christopher was whelped February 10, 1968. His breeder-owner was Joel Marston. A Top Producer in 1971, 1973, 1974, 1975 and 1976, Chris sired a Top Producer, Ch. Starcrest Andy of Lu-Hi and was the grandsire of the all-time Top Producer, Prophet.

Among Chris' get were Top Ten winner Ch. Tsang-Po's Kwai Chu, #9 Chow 1973; Ch. Starcrest Dandy Lion, #8 Chow 1974; Ch. Starcrest Andy of Lu-Hi, #5 Chow 1976; Ch. Starcrest Lemon Drop Kid, the Chow Chow Club's Supreme Chow 1975 and 1976, #4 Non-Sporting Dog 1975 and #2 Non-Sporting Dog 1976.

Chris' paternal grandsire, Jubilee, was a Top Producer with twelve champion get. Chris' forty-seven AKC champion get are out of seventeen dams. Two Top Producers themselves, Ch. Tsang-Po's Ming Lee produced eight and Starcrest Lemon Twist had seven. Eight dams whelped a single champion each.

A superior dog both at stud and in the ring, his breeder-owner-handled record stands as #7 Chow in 1971 and #4 Chow in 1972 and 1973.

Pandee's Hoi Cho Linnchow NA50005 (3/64) Cin.
Sire: Carlee's Imthewon Pandee NA425901 (1/66) Cinnamon
Pandee's Cin Nee Linnchow N680412 (9/63) Cin.
CH. FA-CI CHINKAPIN NB888583 (10/72) Red
Ch. Pagemoor's Tedi-Lee II N768416 (4/63) Red
Dam: Ch. Fa-Ci Cineraria NB329072 (5/70) Red
Dre-Don's Tara Lure NA101731 (4/65) Red

Ch. Fa-Ci Chinkapin was whelped November 25, 1969. His breeder-owner was James R. Facciolli, Jr. of Pennsylvania. A 1974 Top Producer, he sired thirteen AKC champions out of seven dams. Four champion offspring were out of Dre-Don's Dinah Dee. Four dams had a single champion each.

Ch. Audrich's Most Happy Fella NS058578 (5/73)
Red
Sire: Ch. Audrich Tuff Stuff NS132956 (6/75) Red
Ch. Audrich Circe NS033170 (5/73) Red
CH. CABARET CANDY MAN NS216180 (5/76) Red
Ch. Audrich's Black Orpheus NA989333 (11/68)
Black
Dam: Ch. Audrich Star From The East NS158377 (6/75) Black
Ch. Audrich's Cassandra NS033171 (5/74) Red

Ch. Cabaret Candy Man was whelped November 9, 1974. His breeders were Joan and James Richard and his owner Mary Ann Chambers of Illinois. A Top Producr in 1977, Candy Man was out of the Top Producer, Star. Nine dams produced fourteen champions by Candy Man, including a Top Ten winner, Ch. Wah-Hu Redcloud Sugar Daddy, who shattered the all-time Best in Show record for a Chow.

Beamer's Oriental Boi NS048296 (9/73) Red
Sire: Plainacre's Kemo Kim NS150872 (5/75) Red
Plain Acre's Belle Chien NA353746 (12/67) Red
CH. MELODY'S SAINT NOEL NS205527 (1/77) Red
Ch. Lakeview's Chum of Waulee N927256 (5/64) Red
Dam: Plainacre's Pat Tee Kate NS24910 (5/74) Red
Plain Acre's Belle Chien NA353746 (12/67) Red

Ch. Melody's Saint Noel was whelped December 24, 1974. His breeder was Nola Davis and owners Dan and Kim O'Donnell. A Top Producer in 1980, 1981 and 1982, he sired two Top Ten winners: Ch. Checkmate's Indiana Jones, #9 Chow in 1983 and Ch. Claymont's New Edition of Noel, #9 Chow in 1984 and #5 Chow in 1985. Yon's double granddam, Belle Chien, was a Top Producer. An all-breed Best in Show dog and National Specialty winner, Yon was #4 Chow in 1979.

His forty-five AKC champion get are out of nineteen dams. Top Producers themselves, Claymont Lin Chu of Checkmate whelped eight champions and Checkmate's Cherry Brandy produced seven. As a sire, he was eligible for a Silver Certificate as a Producer of Distinction from H.I.S. Publications (Henry and Irene Schlintz).

116

Plainacre's Kemo Kim NS150872 (5/75) Red
Sire: Jemaco Track Twenty-Nine NS262229 (3/79) Red
Ch. Jemaco Fortune Cookie NS181701 (2/76) Red
CH. JONEL'S TRACK MAC TAVISH NS449056 (4/80) Red
Ch. Audrich Angus MacTavish NS101719 (4/77) Black
Dam: Jonel Angelia NS412546 (3/79) Black
Waulee Little One Doll NS060613 (11/73) Red

    Ch. Jonel's Track MacTavish was whelped September 6, 1978. His breeder was Johnie Meador and his owners were Robert and Linda Banghart of California. A 1982 Top Producer, Mac held a show record of having been the #8 Chow in 1983 and #7 Chow in 1984.

    His fifteen AKC champion get were out of six dams. Both Caron's Pantera and Cherie's Reflection O'Chablis produced four champions each. Four other dams had a single champion each.

Ch. Ghat de la Moulaine N507366 (2/60) Red
Sire: Ch. Jean's Leo Lee Lang N977740 (1/65) Red
Ming Wa Ti N314364 (9/60) Red
CH. TSANG-PO'S KWAI CHY N49292 (8/67) Red
Ch. Martonge Jo-Jo of Peke-Chow N762276 (7/63) Red
Dam: Tsang-Po's Miss Lu Jo Lin NA025735 (4/65) Red
Tsang-Po's Miss Lu Ah So N786739 (7/63) Red

Ch. Tsang-Po's Kwai Chy was whelped June 14, 1965. Her breeder was Luther G. Edmondson and her owner was H. A. Allen of Colorado. A 1969 Top Producer, Kwai Chy was the dam of two Top Producers: the breed's all-time Top Producer Ch. Tsang-Po's Ming Lee and Tsang-Po's Autumn Nocturne. Kwai Chy's paternal grandsire and granddam, Ghat and Ming Wa Ti, were Top Producers as well.

Ch. Tsang-Po's Kwai Chy produced thirteen AKC champions out of four litters totaling twenty puppies. Ch. Shanglo's Tishimingo sired nine and Top Producer Ch. Starcrest Mr. Christopher sired the remainder.

Ch. Shanglo's Kodee NA018020 (6/64) Red
Sire: **Ch. Shanglo's Tishimingo NA429505 (8/67) Red**
You Two's Bijou NA138451 (4/65) Red (Holland)
CH. TSANG-PO'S MING LEE NB362337 (9/70) Red
Ch. Jean's Leo Lee Lang N977740 (1/65) Red
Dam: **Ch. Tsang-Po's Kwai Chy N496292 (8/70) Red**
Tsang-Po's Miss Lee Jo Lin NA025735 (4/65) Red

Ch. Tsang-Po's Ming Lee was whelped November 15, 1968. Her breeder was Hal A. Allen and her owners were Dr. and Mrs. Ed North, Jr. A Top Producer in 1973 and 1977, Ming Lee was the daughter of another Top Producer, Kwai Chy. The Top Producer and multi-Best in Show dog Ch. Tsang-Po's Storm Trooper was out of Ming Lee.

Half of Ming Lee's sixteen AKC champions were sired by Top Producer Ch. Starcrest Mr. Christopher. Another five were by the breed's all-time Top Producer, Ch. Don-Lee's Prophet. Ming Lee still holds the title for the most AKC champions produced by a Chow Chow bitch.

Ch. Tsang-Po's Ming Lee was eligible for a Silver Certficate and later a Gold Certificate as a Producer of Distinction from "Show Dogs" magazine.

Duang-Lai de la Moulaine (France)
Sire: Ch. Ghat de la Moulaine N507366 (2/60) Red
Ch. Ychouchanna V. Mongolie (France) Red
KEN-WAN'S TAHG ALONG N649708 (7/62) Red
Ch. Rollie's Chubby Boy N110861 (6/51) Red
Dam: Fluffy Chinese Princess N330176 (10/57) Red
Gotschall's Li Yen N189107 (3/55) Red

Ken-Wan's Tahg Along was whelped January 23, 1961. Her breeder was Mrs. John Showalter and her owners were Mr. and Mrs. William Elster of California. A 1965 Top Producer, she was by the Top Producer Ghat. Tahg Along whelped two Top Producers, Livin' Doll of Poppyland and Ch. Eastward Liontamer of Elster, Liontamer also being a Top Ten winner for the years 1966, 1967, 1969, 1970, 1971 and 1972.

Ken-Wan's Tahg Along whelped a total of twenty-five puppies in five litters sired by Am. Mex. Ch. Starcrest Spy of Poppyland. This resulted in her eight AKC champion offspring.

Ch. Jean's Sammee Tong N579416 (6/62) Red
Sire: Beamer's Beau Chien NA145989 (12/64) Red
Macherie de la Moulaine N766378 (2/63) Red
PLAIN ACRE'S BELLE CHIEN NA353746 (12/67) Red
Beamer's Willie Chum N442416 (3/60) Red
Dam: Beamer's Scarlet Imp N931994 (7/64) Red
Macherie de la Moulaine N766378 (2/63) Red

Plain Acre's Belle Chien was whelped February 19, 1965. Her breeder was Mrs. John Stertz and her owners were C. Williams, Jr. and Manota Stertz of Ohio. A 1968 Top Producer, Belle was the dam of two Top Ten Winners: Ch. Lakeview's Mr. Lu-Kee, #10 Chow in 1971 and #2 Chow in 1972, and Ch. Plain Acre's Char Man Fella, #9 Chow in 1968 and 1969.

The Top Producer Ch. Beamer's Chummy Chinaman sired all nine of Belle Chien's AKC champion produce.

Ch. Pandee's Jubilee NA558428 (4/67) Red
Sire: Starcrest Jupiter of Pandee NA847693 (6/68) Cinn.
Pandee's Zip Orah NA422204 (4/67) Cinnamon
CH. STARCREST BEWITCHED OF HO-SAN NB204135 (1/70) Black
Ch. Starcrest Richard The Lion N494067 (3/61) Red
Dam: Ch. Starcrest Witch Away NA494067 (2/69) Black
Ch. Indian Star's Yu-Lui N883192 (1/65) Black

Ch. Starcrest Bewitched of Ho-San was whelped February 10, 1968. Her breeder was Joel Marston and her owner was Robert Hoo of California. A 1973 Top Producer, she was the granddaughter of the Top Producer Jubilee.

Her mating with the Top Producer Prophet resulted in six of her eight AKC champion offspring.

Ch. Ah Sid's Kyi Chu NA376208 (9/67) Black
Sire: Ch. Starcrest Matinee Idol NB374358 (7/69) Black
Singee-Lee of Wu Paw NA137953 (8/65) Black
STARCREST LEMON TWIST NB566754 (2/71) Cream
Ch. Ghat de la Moulaine N507366 (2/60) Red
Dam: Ch. Sterncrest Jade of Starcrest N677926 (11/63) Red
Poppyland Choo Choo N499341 (2/60) Cream

Starcrest Lemon Twist was whelped May 15, 1969. Her breeder was Joel Marston and her owners were June and Joel Marston of California. A 1974 Top Producer, she was a granddaughter of the Top Producer Ghat. She was also the dam of Ch. Starcrest Lemon Drop Kid, the Chow Chow Club's Supreme Chow in 1975 and 1976 and the #4 and #2 Non-Sporting dog, respectively, for those years.

A total of sixteen puppies whelped in five litters, Lemon Twist produced seven of her eight AKC champions by the top Producer Ch. Starcrest Mr. Christopher.

                                    Ch. Rubilvan's Rebel of Ky-Lin NA296178 (10/65)
                                    Red
                    Sire: Ch. Shang Tai's Sonombre NA686651 (9/67) Red
                                    Ky-Lin's Snow Queen NA095911 (2/66) Black
CH. MASTERPIECE CHATELAINE NS092764 (4/75) Red
                                    Ah Sid Silver Chalice NA797082 (9/67) Blue
                    Dam: Ky-Lin's Resurrection NB231016 (8/70) Red
                                    Ky-Lin's Calliope NA417728 (1/66) Red

Ch. Masterpiece Chatelaine was whelped January 16, 1972. Her breeder was Judith Woodcock and her owner was Barbara Durst of Maryland. A 1978 Top Producer, Chatelaine produced eight AKC champions by two different sires. She was the dam of a Top Ten winner, Ch. Sunswept Tonka.

Ch. Beamer's Chummy Chinaman NA318919 (3/67)
Red
Sire: Ch. Don-Lee's Prophet NB960992 (2/72) Red
Ch. Don-Lee's Jewel of Ho-San NB529757 (7/70)
Red
CH. CHERIE'S CHABLIS O'PROPHET NS143670 (4/75) Cinnamon
Am. Mex. Ch. Starcrest Spy of Poppyland N590368
(9/61) Red
Dam: Don-Lee's Luxury Lace NB727598 (11/73) Cream
Ch. Don-Lee's Jewel of Ho-San NB529757 (7/70)
Red

Ch. Cherie's Chablis O'Prophet was whelped June 18, 1973. Her breeder-owner was Sherrie Harper of California. Chablis was the third generation of Top Producers through her sire Prophet and grandsires Chummy and Spy.

Chablis' son Ch. Cherie's Prince Kim Hi O'Jody was the #2 Chow in 1979 and the Chow Chow Club's Supreme Chow and #10 Non-Sporting dog in 1980. Ch. Cherie's Jubilee of Rebelrun, a Chablis daughter, was the Chow bitch defeating the most Chows for four years in a row.

Ch. Cherie's Chablis O'Prophet produced five litters by five different sires. Four of her nine AKC champion offspring were by Top Producer Ch. Melody's Saint Noel.

Ch. Beamer's Chummy Chinman NA318919 (3/67)
Red
Sire: Ch. Don-Lee's Prophet NB960992 (2/72) Red
Ch. Don-Lee's Jewell of Ho-San NB529757 (7/70)
Red
EL PERRO OZO'S WILD HONEY NS262922 (12/77) Cinnamon
Pandee's Buccaneer NB083042 (7/69) Black
Dam: Pearl's Fan Cee Dander NS090592 (10/74) Cinnamon
Bun-I Pinto Pandee of Poppyland NB841968 (4/72)
Red

El Perro Ozo's Wild Honey was whelped July 19, 1975. Her
breeder-owner was Richard P. Roy of Washington. Wild Honey
was by the breed's all-time Top Producer, Prophet, who was sired by
Top Producer Ch. Beamer's Chummy Chinaman.

Wild Honey was bred back to her sire, Prophet, to produce all
ten of her AKC champion offspring. She was eligible for a Silver
Certificate from "Kennel Review" magazine as a Producer of
Distinction.

**Ch. Beamer's Chummy Chinaman NA318919
(3/67) Red**
Sire: Ch. Don-Lee's Prophet NB9609992 (2/72) Red
**Ch. Don-Lee's Jewel of Ho-San NB529757 (7/70)
Red**
CH. TSANG-PO'S MOTSU INU NS262241 (1/78) Cinnamon
Ch. Starcrest Mr. Christopher NB272998 (7/69) Red
Dam: Ch. Tsang-Po's Lil Bit O'Starcrest NS051095 (4/74) Red
Ch. Tsang-Po's Ming Lee

Ch. Tsang-Po's Motsu Inu was whelped November 2, 1975. Her breeder was Tsang-Po Kennels and she was owned by C. Dunlap. A 1981 Top Producer, she was a third generation Top Producer on her sire's side. Her maternal grandparents, Mr. Christopher and Ming Lee, were also Top Producers. Motsu Inu was the dam of Top Ten winner, Ch. Pinewood Pharoah of Venus, the #6 Chow in 1983.

The Top Producer Ch. Starcrest Surmount sired five of Motsu Inu's eight AKC champions.

Ch. Don-Lee's Prophet NB960992 (2/72) Red
Sire: Ch. Tsang-Po's Bamboo Boy NS29707 (3/77) Cinn.
Ch. Tsang-Po's Lil Bit O'Starcrest NS051095 (4/74) Red

CLAYMONT LIN CHU OF CHECKMATE NS324647 (11/78) Red

Ch. Shamrock's Klan-Cee NS076759 (1/75) Red
Dam: Plainacre's Charman Freebee NS277480 (3/77) Red
Plainacre's Silhouette NS048299 (9/73) Black

Claymont Lin Chu of Checkmate was whelped July 10, 1976. Her breeders were Dan and Kim O'Donnell and her owners were Richard and JoAnne Jaggie of Missouri. A Top Producer in both 1981 and 1982, Lin Chu was the dam of the Top ten winner Ch. Claymont New Edition of Noel, the #9 Chow in 1984 and #5 Chow in 1985.

Her paternal grandsire was the all-time Top Producer, Prophet. The Top Producer Ch. Melody's Saint Noel sired all but one of Lin Chu's eight AKC champion offspring.

Jewell's Oriental Jo-Jo NS169162 (9/75) Red
Sire: Ch. Jewell's Supermanchu NS250184 (6/77) Red
Ch. Jewell's Ti Wo of Tsang-Po's NS137884 Red
CH. PLAINACRE'S WEN SU OF KOBYS NS576686 (1/82) Red
Ch. Shamrock's Klan-Cee NS076759 (1/75) Red
Dam: Plainacre's O'Anni of Sherman NS324541 (7/80) Red
Sherman's Chin Te Fluffy Wun NS0208170 (2/77) Red

Ch. Plainacre's Wen Su of Kobys was whelped June 3, 1980. Her breeders were Robert and Mary Wuest and Manota Stertz, her owners were Steve and Wendy Kobrzycki of Michigan. Both a 1982 and 1985 Top Producer, Wen Su was the dam of a Top Ten winner, Ch. Koby Cassanova of Sweetkins, the #7 Chow in 1982, #5 Chow in 1983 and #3 Chow in 1984.

Wen Su's fourteen AKC champions are from four litters. When bred to the Top Producer Ch. Tsang-Po's Storm Trooper, she produced five champions. Three other sires helped her to produce three champions in each of her other three litters.

Ch. Plainacre's Wen Su of Kobys was eligible for a Silver Certificate as a Producer of Distinction.

The top-winning Chow of all time in England, Ch. Ukwong King Solomon. By B.I.S. Ch. Ukwong Saul of Weircroft x Ukwong Melita. Breeders and owners, Eric and Joan Egerton.

5

The Modern Chow Chow in Other Countries

AMERICANS SEEM to take it for granted that they can buy, sell and breed without restriction. With the exception of Hawaiian quarantine, they travel throughout the United States freely with their dogs. They can import dogs from other countries at will. World Wars have not been fought on American soil

Other countries may not be so fortunate. Stiff quarantine restrictions in some places, especially Sweden and Norway, are discouraging to those who would like to import and usually stressful to the dogs. Battles have been fought in cities and villages, killing and maiming dogs in their wake. Government restrictions during war years have dictated the culling of stock, as food had to be rationed. At times, governments such as the Chinese have banned dogs completely, as they were considered contrary to the ruling power's ideologies.

Britain's Top Stud Dog for the breed, Ch. Minhow Edward of Junggwaw. He was bred by Mr. and Mrs. Stan Smedley and owned by Frank Watkinson.

B.I.S. winner, Ch. Ukwong Adventurer, breeder-owned by Eric Egerton. Sired by Weircroft Venture Boy x T'Saigon Marbella.

England

Descending from the great dogs of the first part of the Twentieth century, Ch. Pusa of Amwell, Ch. Lemning, Ch. Akbar, Champions Choonam Brilliantine and Brilliantina, Ch. Pu Yi of Amwell, Ch. Choonam Hung Kwong and Rochow Champions Dragoon and Adjutant, came a new era of Chows and dedicated Chowists.

The Ukwong Kennel of Eric and Joan Egerton has seen one record-setting Chow after another pass through its gates. Having begun with a Talifu bitch from Mrs. J. Boot, the Egertons' dogs have included such distinguished ones as: Best in Show Int. Ch. Chang Shi Ukwong, the #2 all-time Top Sire in England and the dog whose name the Comtesse de Changy allowed the Egertons to use as their kennel name; B.I.S. Ch. Fairwood Fu Simba, the #3 Top Sire; B.I.S. Int. Ch. Emperor of Junggwaw, the litter brother to Frank Watkinson's Ch. Minhow Edward of Junggwaw, the breed's #1 Sire; B.I.S. Int. Ch. Astom, whom they co-owned with the Comtesse de Changy; B.I.S. Int. Ch. Illustrious Lad of Ukwong; Ch. Weircroft Saul of Ukwong and Saul's son, the record-breaking Ch. Ukwong King Solomon. King Solomon, or Solly, was twice England's Dog of the Year and was the winner of multiple Chow of the Year shows. The Ukwong Kennel disbanded once, regrouped and now is taking it easy as Joan and Eric travel back and forth between England and the United States for judging assignments.

The Junggwaw Kennel of Mr. and Mrs. Stan Smedley is best known for the three champions Emperor, Edward and Enrico of Junggwaw.

Miss C. E. Collett, Chow author and owner of Barwick Chows, produced the dam of the aforementioned Junggwaw litter, Phillida of Barwick and contributed to many kennels' growth.

The Talifu Kennel of Mrs. Boot produced England's Top Brood Bitch, Tinkerbelle of Talifu. Her four champion offspring earned her that honor.

Besides the distinction of owning England's Top Sire, Ch. Minhow Edward of Junggwaw, Frank Watkinson's Minhow Kennel produced a special dog, Ch. Minhow Martino, the holder of over two dozen Challenge Certificates.

Edna, Len and Carol Entwisle, Edlen Chows, were known for their Solly daughter, Ch. Edlen Crisandra. Crisandra was Top Puppy of the Year, all breeds, in 1973.

At the end of each year, there usually is one Top Winning Chow. However, in 1981, a dog and a bitch acquired an equal number of points. The bitch is Ch. Baytor Flossie Flump, by Ch. Baytor Sasha x Baytor Winter Gold, breeder-owned by Anita Westlake. *D.A. Lewis*

Baytor Kennel is one of the largest Chow kennels in England. The Westlakes often enter as many as seven dogs at championship shows. Here we see (from left) Baytor Bitter Sweet, Kyong Katmandoo of Yama at Baytor, Baytor Blue Cobweb and Baytor Sister Kate. *D.A. Lewis*

The Top Winning Chow in 1982, Ch. Weircroft Sir Giles. Bred by Ivy Bancroft and owned by Mrs. J. Owens, he is by Sheshoon Santa Fe x Weircroft Christmas Joy. Giles is pictured just after he bested 128 entries at the Northern Counties Chow Chow Club Championship show judged by Paul Odenkirchen.

D.A. Lewis

B.I.S. winner, Ch. Tiko Ling of Hanoi, breeder-owned by Dulcie Smith. He is by Ch. Wongtung's Chang of Canton x Ch. Kwong Kee of Silverway.

Other kennels active in recent years have been: Westwood, Mrs. Stanley Barrett; Wongtung, Mrs. E. Downborough; Mulfra, W. Scriven and Siverway, Mabel Bird. Mrs. Brind, Brinchow, produced Ch. Una-So-Sweet. The Termade Kennel of the Terry Wrights was noted for Ch. Termade Renata who was Best of Breed at the Chow Chow Club show. The Chow author Lydia Ingleton was known for her Kin-Shan Chows which won for both her and the Chowists around the world who imported them. Mr. E. A. Burrows, Penhow, has had considerable success with smooth Chows.

Arthur and Anita Westlake established the Baytor Chows and were long recognized for a fine string of winners, including many blues. Anita Westlake was the breeder-owner of Ch. Westlake Flossie Flump who tied for the Top Winning Chow honor in 1981. The Top Winning Chow in 1983, Ch. Baytor Blue Star, was owned and bred by Anita.

Mrs. Dulcie Smith, Hanoi, is known for the Best in Show winner Ch. Tiko Ling of Hanoi. She was also the breeder-owner of Ch. Hanoi Man Friday, the dog who tied with Flossie Flump for the Top Winning Chow honors in 1981.

Mrs. Ivy Bancroft, Weircroft, was the breeder of the Top Winning Chow in 1982, Ch. Weircroft Sir Giles. She also bred Ch. Weircroft Saul of Ukwong whom she sent to the Egertons as pick of the litter.

The 1984 Chow of the Year Show drew an entry of some 235 Chows. It was topped by an eighteen-mohth-old bitch, Ch. Taysmith Tia Dora of Tanlap. She was bred by Mrs. J. Taylor and owned by Mrs. S. Jakeman.

The Top Winning Chow in Great Britain in 1984 and 1985 was Ch. Fort Knox Here's the Tiger at Towmena. His owner, Rodney Oldham, Towmena Kennels, imported him from his Swedish breeder, Mrs. A. C. Ekengren.

The Top Winning Chow in 1986, Ch. Mr. Christian, was also the top winning dog in the Utility Group that year. His breeders and owners were Mr. and Mrs. P. Westley.

Canada

The much-decorated war hero W. A. "Billy" Bishop pioneered Chows in Canada. In the days when the breed was a rarity, he had several. The uniqueness of the breed, coupled with his celebrity status, drew interest. It is probable that any offspring he bred

The Top Winning Chow in both 1984 and 1985, Ch. Fort Knox Here's The Tiger at Towmena. Sired by Nor. and Swed. Ch. Fort Knox Where's The Tiger x Swed. Ch. Ukwong Angel of Taibel.   *D.A. Lewis*

Not only the Top Winning Chow in 1986, but also the Top Winning Dog in the Utility Group that year, Ch. Mr. Christian. His sire was Sheshoon Santa Fe and his dam, Betanmel Ho-Che-Cha-Nia.   *D.A. Lewis*

Air Marshall W.A. (Billy) Bishop with three English imports. The original Chow Chow Club of Canada's founding can be credited to the efforts of this man.

Head study of B.I.S. winner, Ch. Mi-Pao's Bandera. Breeder-owner, Paul Odenkirchen.

Ch. Djimat van de Martin-Hoeve, bred in Holland by the Martins, sired by Kwan-Ti van de Tongelreep out of Heliam, and owned by Paul Odenkirchen who bred him to Ch. Soekaa to produce the puppy pictured, Can. Am. Ch. Mi-Pao's Hidje-Ti Sarewoe who was owned by Betty Schellenberg in the USA.

B.I.S. winner, Can. Am. Ch. Mi-Pao's Timang. By Hi-Bo's Adiraja x
Mi-Tan's Istri-Ganti and breeder-owned by Paul Odenkirchen.

One of the foundation sires used at Mi Pao, Int. Ch. Chang-Shi Hong-
Kwong, bred by Belgian Comtesse Mary de Changy. He was by Int. and
Eng. Ch. Astom x Chang-Shi Fat-Ima.

eventually ended up in the homes of friends. Billy Bishop helped form the Chow Chow Club of Canada.

Around 1930, two kennels finally appeared to be active in the Ontario region, Ku and Yan-Kee. The Chia Win Chows from Michigan began crossing the border to be exhibited and sold. Mrs. Yan Paul had early winners for her Suyan Kennel with Chia Win stock.

Walter Kenyon, Chalfont Chow Kennel, was president of the CCC of Canada in the mid-forties and later served as an historian of Canadian Chowdom. The first Canadian-bred Best in Show Chow was Gwendolin Kenyon's Ch. Winnitoba's Rusty Waun.

During this time the Marhal, Nor-Ton, Ho Han and Tohio kennels in the States were exhibiting in or exporting to Canada where there was a growing fancy and a demand for stock.

M. Joey Nattrass began her Chi-Kwang Kennel in 1946. At one time, she was the kennel manager of the Foo H'sing Kennel and provided them with some foundation stock. Joey was editor and publisher of the international breed magazine "The Chow Chow Newsletter" which was founded in 1959. She also had the distinction of breeder-owner-handling the first Chow to go Best Puppy in Show.

The root of the Mi-Pao Kennel, Reg. of F.P.A. and Minnie Odenkirchen can partially be credited to Minnie's grandmother, Mrs. W. S. M. Kloos-Dixon who was the founder of the Dutch Chow Chow Club in the forties. In the late fifties, Paul and a pair of Chows arrived in Canada a couple of months before Minnie, who waited in Holland. By 1960 their breeding program had begun. They based their kennel on stock from Loumi-Hoeve, Mongolie, Chang-Shi, Tongelreep, Kou Ling and Martin-Hoeve. These Dutch, Belgian and English types were combined into a type Mi-Pao became noted for. Specialty and all-breed wins were frequent for the Mi-Pao dogs in both the United States and Canada. Exports to other countries did well, too. Paul has judged in many countries and has participated in several breed standard committees. Thus, he is a rare individual who has had a view of the Chow, its good features and bad, the world over.

The Foo H'sing Kennel of Madge P. Wiseman sported many a winner. The multi-Best in Show Ch. Foo H'sing's Fu Tu was the Top Winning Chow for five years in the sixties. Mrs. Wiseman also imported Minhow Miss Sadie Wu from England and made her a champion and Top Producer in Canada.

Multiple Canadian and American B.I.S. winner, Can. Am. Ch. Mi-Tu's Han-Su Shang. He is owned by Herb and Joan Williams and Fred Peddie, of Toronto. "Shang" was Canada's Top Dog for 1975 and holds the world record for Chow Chow Best in Show wins. Here he shares the spotlight with his daughter, Poppy.

The Top Winning Chow in Canada for five years, Ch. Foo H'sing's Fu-Tu was handled to multiple Bests in Show by Joey Nattrass for owners Mr. and Mrs. A. Garwood and breeder, Mrs. Weisman.

A multi-B.I.S. and Specialty B.O.B. winner, Ch. Taichung Justin of Mike Mar.

The 1985 Supreme Chow in Canada, Am. Can. Ch. Jasam's Temujin. Sired by Am. Can. Ch. Taichung Justin of Mike-Mar x Ch. Jasam's Topaz from Taichung.

The Mi-Tu Kennel of Pat and Russ Robb is most recognized for having produced the noted winner Am. Can. Ch. Mi-Tu's Han Su Shang. Margaret R. Crisson's Criscoken Chows have done well in both Canada and the United States. Additionally, her dogs have earned a number of obedience titles. (See the chapter on Chows in Obedience.) Gail Forsythe, Lionheart Chows, Reg., had the Top Winning bitch, Ch. Liontamer Lightheart in 1976.

The Bu Dynasty Kennel, formerly called Lidice, belongs to Herb and Joan Williams and John C. Frederick Peddie. In their many owner-handled victories, the multiple Best in Show Ch. Foo H'sing Mister Linn Wu was one of their earliest winners. Am. Can. Ch. Mi-Tu's Han Su Shang was a multiple Best in Show winner in both Canada and the United States. Shang also won the National in the United States twice. In 1979, he was Supreme Chow here. From 1974 through 1977, Shang was Canada's Top Winning Chow. Bu Dynasty bred and co-owned Ch. Bu Dynasty the Stylist who was in the American Top Ten in 1980 and Supreme Chow in 1981. Another winner of theirs was Ch. Hanoi Tiko Topper who won the Chow Chow Club National in the United States in 1977.

John A. and Sandra A. Post, Jasam, Reg., showed their Am. Can. Ch. Jasam's Temujin to Best of Breed at the 1985 Chow Chow Fanciers of Canada National Specialty. Temujin was Supreme Chow Chow in Canada in 1985 and was in the Top Three in 1986.

Hanna Kuester filled her Hanchow Kennel not only with the most lovely specimens she could buy or breed, but also with homely, cast-off waifs she rescued simply because they were Chow Chows. There will rarely be found a Chowist as devoted as Hanna. To her, the love of her dogs came first and the winning was incidental.

The Lioning Chows of Nancy Meisner and Samuel Henning began in 1978. To date, they have bred fifteen champions, five of which have taken group placements. They have had particular success with Ch. Lioning Handsome who was Top Chow Puppy and #2 Chow in Canada in 1984 with four Best Puppy in Show awards. That year he was also Chow Chow of the Year, meaning he defeated the greatest number of Chows. Handsome was the #1 Chow in Canada and Chow Chow of the Year in 1985. In 1986, he was the #3 Chow and again Chow Chow of the Year. He has taken Best of Breed at the esteemed Club VI Specialty four times and won a Specialty Best of Breed and Group I there in 1985.

Other known kennels of Canada include: Sinkiang, Neil and Rose MacEachern; Paradox, Dr. Joan Bach; Chan Lan, Reg.,

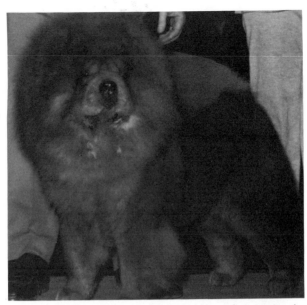

Ch. Lioning Handsome won the 1986 Canadian National Specialty under judge Mrs. G. Wanner, handled by Samuel Henning for breeder-owner Nancy Meisner.   *J. Raymond*

The bitch, Ch. Lioning Sunburst, Best Puppy in Show at Guelph K.C. championship show. Sire, Ch. Lioning Handsome; dam, Lioning Dainty Doll and breeder-owner, Nancy Meisner.   *A. Smith*

Ch. Djimat van de Martin-Hoeve, by Kwan-Ti van de Tongelreep x Heliam. Bred by Mr. and Mrs. Martin (Holland). Owner, F.P.A. Odenkirchen.

A multiple Best Puppy in Show bitch, Ch. Nawshi's Luba Lee, breeder-owner-handled by Audrey Dobrowney for co-owner Dr. Murray Wade. By Ch. Mi-Pao's The Graduate x Mi-Pao's Miss Scarlett.

146

Beverly Britnell; Taipan Chow Chows, Mona J. Cotie; Von Casumar, Marge Ste. Marie; Champad Kennels, Barbara Kristoff and Kin-Chi, Helen and Doug Schwoob.

Other successful exhibitors in recent years have been: Bert and Carol Straus, Judith Tulloch, Dr. Gordon Mills, Audrey Dobrowney and Dr. Murray Wade.

Canada's Top Winning Chow Chow—1960-1985 — Including Breed, Group and Best in Show Wins

1960	Ch. Chi-Kwang's Gib-Tay
1961	Can. Am. Ch. Loy-Jean's China Boi
1962	Ch. Mi-Pao's Djoeragan Toean
1963	Ch. Nor-Ton's Canadian Moon (B)
1964	Ch. Foo H'sing's Fu-Tu
1965	Ch. Foo H'sing's Fu-Tu
1966	Ch. Foo H'sing's Fu-Tu
1967	Ch. Foo H'sing's Fu-Tu
1968	Ch. Foo H'sing's Fu-Tu
1969	Ch. Mi-Pao's Oetara
1970	Ch. Ai Wong Chee
1971	Ch. Foo H'sing's Mister Linn Wu
1972	Can. Am. Ch. Mi-Pao's Timang
1973	Ch. Mi-Pao's Bandera
1974	Can. Am. Ch. Mi-Tu's Han Su Shang
1975	Can. Am. Ch. Mi-Tu's Han Su Shang
1976	Can. Am. Ch. Mi-Tu's Han Su Shang
1977	Can. Am. Ch. Mi-Tu's Han Su Shang
1978	Can. Am. Bda. Ch. Starcrest Surmount
1979	Can. Am. Ch. Mi-Tu's Han Su Shang
1980	Can. Am. Ch. Bu Dynasty's The Royalist
1981	Can. Am. Ch. Bu Dynasty's Shang Hi
1982	Can. Am. Ch. Bu Dynasty's Shang Hi
1983	Can. Am. Ch. Bu Dynasty's Shang Hi
1984	Can. Am. Ch. Taichung Justin of Mike-Mar
1985	Ch. Lioning Handsome

Canada's Top Winning Chow Bitch—1960-1985

1960	Ch. Chi-Kwang's Su Ling
1961	Ch. Chi-Kwang's Su Ling
1962	Ch. U'Kwong's Red Queen
1963	Ch. Norton's Canadian Moon
1964	Kin-Chi's Tien Tay
1965	Ch. Minhow Miss Sadie Wu
1966	Kin-Chi's Cee Cee
1967	Ch. Kin-Chi's Miss-Te-Fu

1968	Ch. Saymar Sabrina
1969	Empress Ai Chu Chi and Ch. Van Rhoeden's Kan-dy
1970	Ky-Lin's Queen Bee of Marbob
1971	Ch. Mi-Tu's Tien How
1972	Ch. Mi-Tu's Mai Mai
1973	Ch. Mi-Pao's Mallam
1974	Ch. Mi-Pao's Belia
1975	Yantan's China Bear
1976	Ch. Liontamer Lightheart
1977	Ch. Spindrift's Miss Cuddle Bear
1978	Ch. Bu Dynasty's Mandy of Helena
1979	Ch. Wah-Hu's Red Satin Dancer
1980	Ch. Hsi Wang's Song Sumi
1981	Ch. Bam Bam O'Cambellyn
1982	Can. Am. Ch. Paradox Tiko Rose
1983	Bu Dynasty's The African Queen
1984	Ebony Mist of Prairie View
1985	Stardust Dakota Gold

Canada's Chow Chow of the Year—1979-1985

(The Chow defeating the greatest number of Chows.)

1979	Can. Am. Ch. Mi-Tu's Han Su Shang
1980	Can. Am. Ch. Bu Dynasty's The Royalist
1981	Can. Am. Ch. Bu Dynasty's The Royalist
1982	Can. Am. Ch. Chi-Debut's Nutcracker Suite
1983	Jen-Lu's Pekin Tai Pan
1984	Ch. Lioning Handsome
1985	Ch. Lioning Handsome

Canada's Supreme Chow of the Year—1970-1985

(The Chow with the highest average of Chows defeated divided by the number of wins.)

1970	Ch. Kin-Chi's Ku-Sa
1971	Ch. Kin-Chi's Ku-Sa
1972	Ch. Ai Wong Chee
1973	Ch. Kin-Chi's Ku-Sa
1974	Can. Am. Ch. Mi-Tu's Mai Mai
1975	Ch. Sinkiang's Wu Sabu
1976	Ch. Criscoken's Allegiant
1977	Can. Am. Ch. Hillcastle Lon Don
1978	Can. Am. Ch. Mi-Tu's Han Su Shang
1979	Can. Am. Ch. Mi-Tu's Han Su Shang
1980	Ch. Hsi Wang's Song Sumi (B)
1981	Ch. Hsi Wang's Song Sumi (B)
1982	Can. Am. Ch. Paradox Tiko Rose (B)
1983	Mi-Tu's Moon Mist and San Gates Hsi Yin Shuang
1984	Ch. Mi-Pao's Viking
1985	Ch. Jasam's Temujin

Ch. Merah van de Loumi-Hoeve, bred by Lou Huyen (Holland). By Han-Tie Bambus x Rosanne. Owner, Paul Odenkirchen.

Ch. Mongo van Mongolie, bred and owned by Henk van de Wouw (Holland). By Ch. Alexis of Adel x Anoz van Mongolie.

Ch. Ki-Dong King (Holland), grandsire of Ch. Ghat de la Moulaine. Owner, Henk van de Wouw. Pictured at eleven years of age.

Nat. and Int. Ch. Koeblai-Khan-Tiong-Bwa, "The Professor," by Pandee's New World Ambassador x Cinderella van de Burghardt. Owner, Henk van de Wouw (Holland).

Nat. and Int. Ch. Kuang-Wu of Liang-Ming-Keou, by Mi-Ka-Lo v.d. Loumi-Hoeve x Joengkai v.d. Loumi-Hoeve. Breeder-owner, H. Steegmans.

Nat. and Int. Ch. Kai-Men-Ti Liweng, descendent of Ch. Chang-Shi Uk-wong and Choonam bloodlines. Owner, H.B. Wachholtz.   *Clif*

151

B.I.S. winner, Polish Ch. Mi-Pao's Matjan, by Int. Ch. Chang-Shi Hong Kwong x Ch. Tiga. Breeder, P. Odenkirchen. Owner, Zygmunt Jakubowski (Poland).

(Top) Ho-Ty von Meh-Thue, bred by Erich Buchner (Germany). (Left) Mi-Pao's Poetri, bred by Paul Odenkirchen (Canada). (Right) Zena of Junggwaw, bred by Stan Smedley (England). Owner, Martha Visser, You-Two Kennels (Holland).

Jap. Ch. Ki-Hoo's Black Panther of Cad, black male by Eng. Ch. Ukwong Mr. Moses x Raphsody of Cad. Breeder-owner, Mr. Hiro Takagi (Japan).

Holland

The Dutch breeders have faced one adversity after another. War ripped through their land, major kennels have lost all stock to infection and the Chow's popularity soared, then suffered, during a fad period. Still, a few prominent kennels are credited with shaping the history of the Chow in Holland: Golliwogs, Mrs. F. Geitel de Lange; van de Doorwerth, Mrs. Roes; Wamchow, Mrs. Lamerus; Go-Chow, Mr. and Mrs. Oswald; You-Two, Martha Visser; Liang-Ming-Keou, Mr. H. Steegmans; Tongelreep, Mr. van de Broek; van Majodo, Mr. and Mrs. J. Doll; Kai-Men-Ti, Mrs. H. Wahholtz; Loumi-Hoeve, Lou and Miep Nuyen; Ki-Dong, Kitty van Dong and Henk van de Wouw who together have produced the great van Mongolie Chows.

Other Countries

The foregoing pictures are but a smattering of mostly exported dogs. However, their destinations have been to places where there is a definite Chow fancy, however small it might be. The Japanese, for instance, have imported stock from bloodlines all over the world and breeders there are now able to make compatible matings themselves. However, they are still willing to scout for more dogs that will prove beneficial to the further development of the breed in their country.

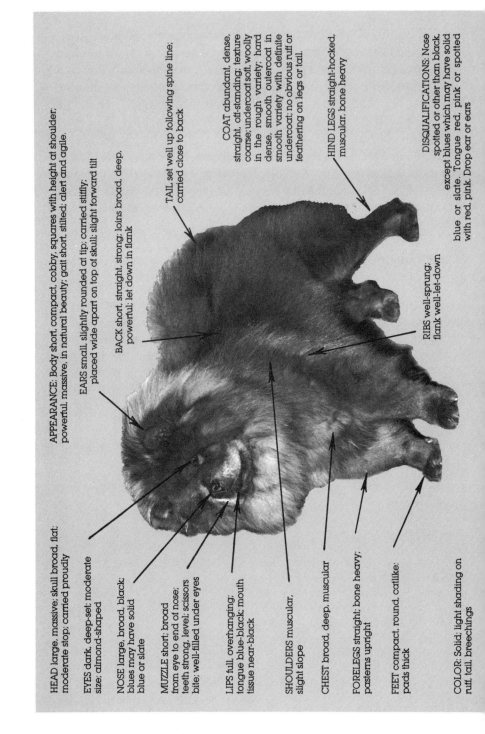

HEAD large, massive; skull broad, flat; moderate stop; carried proudly

EYES dark, deep-set; moderate size; almond-shaped

NOSE large, broad, black; blues may have solid blue or slate

MUZZLE short; broad from eye to end of nose; teeth strong, level; scissors bite; well-filled under eyes

LIPS full, overhanging; tongue blue-black; mouth tissue near-black

SHOULDERS muscular, slight slope

CHEST broad, deep, muscular

FORELEGS straight; bone heavy; pasterns upright

FEET compact, round, catlike; pads thick

COLOR: Solid; light shading on ruff, tail breechings

APPEARANCE: Body short, compact, cobby; squares with height at shoulder; powerful, massive, in natural beauty; gait short, stilted; alert and agile.

EARS small, slightly rounded at tip; carried stiffly; placed wide apart on top of skull; slight forward tilt

BACK short, straight, strong; loins broad, deep, powerful; let down in flank

TAIL set well up following spine line; carried close to back

COAT abundant, dense, straight, off-standing; texture coarse; undercoat soft, woolly in the rough variety; hard dense, smooth outercoat in smooth variety with definite undercoat; no obvious ruff or feathering on legs or tail

HIND LEGS straight-hocked, muscular, bone heavy

RIBS well-sprung; flank well-let-down

DISQUALIFICATIONS: Nose spotted or other than black, except blues which may have solid blue or slate. Tongue red, pink or spotted with red, pink. Drop ear or ears

6

The Chow Chow Standards

T HE CHOW CHOW CLUB, INC. sought to clarify the official Standard that had been in existence since March 11, 1941. The resultant effort of a committee of world-renowned Chowists and the general membership was approved by The American Kennel Club on November 11, 1986. The revised Standard allows for the smooth coated variety and defines more characteristics that should be considered serious faults.

Characteristics

An ancient breed of northern Chinese origin, this all-purpose dog of China was used for hunting, herding, pulling and protection of the home. While primarily a companion today, his working origin must always be remembered when assessing true Chow type.

General Appearance

A powerful, sturdy, squarely built, upstanding dog of Arctic type, medium size with strong muscular development and heavy bone. The body is compact, short coupled, broad and deep, the tail set high and carried close to the back, the whole supported by four straight, strong, sound legs. Viewed from the side, the hind legs have little apparent angulation and the hock joint and metatarsals are directly beneath the hip joint. It is this structure which produces the characteristic short, stilted gait unique to the breed. The large head with broad, flat skull and short, broad and deep muzzle is proudly carried and accentuated by a ruff. Elegance and substance must be combined into a well balanced whole, never so massive as to outweigh his ability to be active, alert and agile. Clothed in a smooth or an offstanding rough double coat, the Chow is a masterpiece of beauty, dignity and naturalness, unique in his blue-black tongue, scowling expression and stilted gait.

Head

Skull and Stop—proudly carried, large in proportion to the size of the dog but never so exaggerated as to make the dog seem top heavy or to result in a low carriage. The top skull is broad and flat from side to side and front to back. Coat and loose skin cannot substitute for the correct bone structure. Viewed in profile, the toplines of the muzzle and skull are approximately parallel, joined by a moderate stop. The padding of the brows may make the stop appear steeper than it is.

Muzzle—the muzzle is short in comparison to the length of the top skull but never less than one-third of the head length. The muzzle is broad and well filled out under the eyes, its width and depth are equal and both dimensions should appear to be the same from its base to its tip. This square appearance is achieved by correct bone structure plus padding of the muzzle and full cushioned lips. The muzzle should never be so padded or cushioned as to make it appear other than square in shape. The upper lips completely cover the lower lips when the mouth is closed but should not be pendulous.

Nose—large, broad and black in color with well opened nostrils. *Disqualifying Fault*—nose spotted or distinctly other color than black, except in blue Chows which may have solid blue or slate noses.

Mouth and Tongue—edges of the lips black, tissues of the mouth mostly black, gums preferably black. A solid black mouth is ideal. The top surface and edges of the tongue a solid blue-black, the darker the better. *Disqualifying Fault*—the top surface or edges of the tongue red or pink or with one or more spots of red or pink.

Teeth—strong and even with a scissors bite.

Eyes—dark brown, deep set and placed wide apart and obliquely, of moderate size, almond in shape. The correct placement should create an Oriental appearance. The eye rims black with lids which neither turn in nor droop and the pupils of the eyes clearly visible. *Serious Faults*—entropion or ectropion, or pupils wholly or partially covered by loose skin.

Ears—small, moderately thick, triangular in shape with a slight rounding at the tip, carried stiffly erect but with a slight forward tilt. Placed wide apart with the inner corner on top of the skull. An ear which flops as the dog moves is very undesirable. *Disqualifying Fault*—drop ear or ears. A drop ear is one which breaks at any point from its base to its tip or which is not carried stiffly erect but lies parallel to the top of the skull.

Expression—essentially scowling, dignified, lordly, sober and snobbish, one of independence. The scowl is achieved by a marked brow with a padded button of skin just above the inner, upper corner of each eye; by sufficient play of skin to form frowning brows and a distinct furrow between the eyes beginning at the base of the muzzle and extending up the forehead; by the correct ear shape, carriage and placement. Excessive loose skin is not desirable. Wrinkles on the muzzle do not contribute to expression and are not required.

Neck and Body

Neck—strong, full, well muscled, nicely arched and of sufficient length to carry the head proudly above the topline when standing at attention.

Body—short, compact, close coupled, strongly muscled, broad, deep and well let down in the flank.

Topline—straight, strong and level from the withers to the root of the tail.

Chest—broad, deep and muscular, never narrow or slab-sided. The ribs close together and well sprung, not barrel. The spring of the front ribs is somewhat narrowed at their lower ends to permit the shoulder and upper arm to fit smoothly against the chest wall. The floor of the chest is broad and deep extending down to the tips of the elbows. The point of sternum slightly in front of the shoulder points. *Serious Faults*—labored or abdominal breathing (not to include normal panting), narrow or slab-sided chest.

Loin—well muscled, strong, short, broad and deep.

Croup—short and broad with powerful rump and thigh muscles giving a level croup. The body, back, coupling and croup must all be short to give the required square build.

Tail—well feathered, set high and carried closely to the back at all times, following the line of the spine at the start.

Forequarters

Shoulders—strong, well muscled, the tips of the shoulder blades moderately close together; the spine of the shoulder forms an angle of approximately 55 degrees with the horizontal and forms an angle with the upper arm of approximately 110 degrees resulting in less reach of the forelegs. Length of upper arm never less than length of shoulder blade. Elbow joints set well back alongside the chest wall, elbows turning in nor out.

Forelegs—perfectly straight from elbow to foot with heavy bone which must be in proportion to the rest of the dog. Viewed from the front, the forelegs are parallel and widely spaced commensurate with the broad chest.

Pasterns—short and upright. Wrists shall not knuckle over.

Feet—round, compact, cat-like, standing well up on the thick toe pads. The dewclaws may be removed.

Hindquarters

The rear assembly broad, powerful, and well muscled in the hips and thighs, heavy in bone with rear and front bone approximately equal. Viewed from the rear, the legs are straight, parallel and widely spaced commensurate with the broad pelvis.

Stifle Joint—shows little angulation, is well knit and stable, points straight forward and the bones of the joint should be clean and sharp.

Hock Joint—well let down and appears almost straight. The hock joint must be strong, well knit and firm, never bowing or breaking forward or to either side. The hock joint and the

160

metatarsals lie in a straight line below the hip joint. *Serious Faults*—unsound stifle or hock joints.

Metatarsals—short and perpendicular to the ground.

Feet—same as front.

Coat

There are two types of coat: rough and smooth. Both are double coated.

Rough—in the rough coat, the outer coat is abundant, dense, straight and offstanding, rather coarse in texture; the undercoat soft, thick and wooly. Puppy coat soft, thick and wooly overall. The coat forms a profuse ruff around the head and neck, framing the head. The coat and ruff generally longer in dogs than in bitches. The coat length varies markedly on different Chows and thickness, texture and condition should be given greater emphasis than length. Obvious trimming or shaping is undesirable. Trimming of the whiskers, feet and metatarsals optional.

Smooth—the smooth coated Chow is judged by the same standard as the rough coated Chow except that references to the quantity and distribution of the outer coat are not applicable to the smooth coated Chow, which has a hard, dense, smooth outer coat with a definite under coat. There should be no obvious ruff or feathering on the legs or tail.

Color

Clear coated, solid or solid with lighter shadings in the ruff, tail and featherings. There are five colors in the Chow: red (light golden to deep mahogany), black, blue, cinnamon (light fawn to deep cinnamon) and cream. Acceptable colors to be judged on an equal basis.

Gait

Proper movement is the crucial test of proper conformation and soundness. It must be sound, straight moving, agile, brief, quick and powerful, never lumbering. The rear gait short and stilted because of the straighter rear assembly. It is from the side that the unique stilted action is most easily assessed. The rear leg moves up and forward from the hip in a straight, stilted pendulum-like line with a slight bounce in the rump, the legs extend neither far forward nor far backward. The hind foot has a strong thrust which transfers power to the body in an almost straight line due to the minimal rear leg angulation. To transmit this power efficiently to the front assembly, the coupling must be short and there should be no roll through the midsection. Viewed from the rear, the line of bone from hip joint to pad remains straight as the dog moves. As the speed increases the hindlegs incline slightly inward. The stifle joints must point in the line of travel, not outward resulting in a bowlegged appearance nor hitching in under the dog. Viewed from the front, the line of bone from shoulder joint to pad remains straight as the dog moves. As the speed increases, the forelegs do not move in exact parallel planes, rather, incline slightly inward. The front legs must not swing out in semi-circles nor mince or show any evidence of hackney action. The front and rear assemblies must be in dynamic equilibrium. Somewhat lacking in speed, the Chow has excellent endurance because the sound, straight rear leg provides direct, usable power efficiently.

Size and Proportions

Size—the average height of adult specimens is 17 to 20 inches at the withers but in every case consideration of overall proportions and type should take precedence over size.

Proportions—square in profile and close coupled. Distance from forechest to point of buttocks equals height at the highest points of the withers. *Serious Faults*—profile other than square. Distance from tip of elbow to ground is half the height at the withers. Floor of chest level with tips of elbows. Width viewed from the front and rear is the same and must be broad. It is these proportions that are essential to true Chow type. In judging puppies, no allowance should be made for their failure to conform to these proportions.

Temperament

Keen intelligence, an independent spirit and innate dignity give the Chow an aura of aloofness. It is the Chow's nature to be reserved and discerning with strangers. Displays of aggression or timidity are unacceptable. Because of its deep set eyes the Chow has limited peripheral vision and is best approached within the scope of that vision.

Summary

Faults shall be penalized in proportion to the deviation from the standard. In judging the Chow, the overall picture is of primary consideration. Exaggeration of any characterisic at the expense of balance or soundness shall be severely penalized. Equally objectionable are snipey, fine boned specimens and overdone, ponderous, cloddy specimens. In comparing specimens of different sex, due allowance must be made in favor of the bitches who may not have as much head or substance as do the males. There is an impression of femininity in bitches as compared to an impression of masculinity in dogs. Type should include general appearance, temperament, the harmony of all parts, and soundness especially as seen when the dog is in motion. There should be proper emphasis on movement which is the final test of the Chow's conformation, balance and soundness.

DISQUALIFICATIONS

Nose spotted or distinctly other color than black, except in blue Chows which may have solid blue or slate noses.

The top surface or edges of the tongue red or pink or with one or more spots of red or pink.

Drop ear or ears. A drop ear is one which breaks at any point from its base to its tip or which is not carried stiffly erect but lies parallel to the top of the skull.

The English Standard for the Chow Chow

GENERAL APPEARANCE—Active, compact, short coupled and essentially well balanced, leonine in appearance, proud, dignified bearing; well knit frame, tail carried well over the back.

CHARACTERISTICS—Quiet dog, good guard, bluish black tongue, unique in its stilted gait.

TEMPERAMENT—Independent, loyal yet aloof.

HEAD AND SKULL—Skull flat, broad; stop not pronounced, well filled out under eyes. Muzzle moderate in length, broad from eyes to end (not pointed at end like a fox). Nose, large and wide in all cases, black (with exception of cream and near white in which case a light-coloured nose is permissible, and in blues and fawns a self-coloured nose).

163

EYES—Dark, almond shaped, fairly small and clean. A matching coloured eye permissible in blue and fawns. Clean eye, free from entropion, never being penalized for sake of mere size.

EARS—Small, thick, slightly rounded at tip, carried stiffly and wide apart but tilting well forward over the eyes and slightly towards each other, giving peculiar characteristic scowling expression of the breed. Scowl never to be achieved by loose wrinkled skin of head.

MOUTH—Teeth strong and level, jaws strong, with perfect, regular and complete scissor bite, i.e., the upper teeth closely overlapping the lower teeth and set square to the jaws. Tongue bluish black. Roof of mouth and flews black (blue black), gums preferably black.

NECK—Strong, full not short, set well on shoulders and slightly arched.

FOREQUARTERS—Shoulders muscular and sloping. Forelegs perfectly straight, of moderate length, with good bone.

BODY—Chest broad and deep. Ribs well sprung but not barrelled. Back short, level and strong. Loins powerful.

HINDQUARTERS—Hindlegs muscular, hocks well let down, with minimal angulation, essential to produce characteristic stilted gait. From hocks downwards to appear straight, hocks never flexing forward.

FEET—Small, round, cat-like, standing well on toes.

TAIL—Set high, carried well over back.

GAIT/MOVEMENT—Short and stilted. Forelegs and hindlegs moving parallel to each other and straight forward.

COAT—Either rough or smooth.
- (a) Rough—profuse, abundant, dense, straight and stand-off. Outer coat rather coarse in texture, with soft wooly undercoat. Especially thick round neck forming mane or ruff with good culottes or breechings on back of thighs.
- (b) Smooth—coat short, abundant, dense, straight, upstanding not flat, plush-like in texture.

Any artificial shortening of the coat which alters the natural outline or expression should be penalized.

COLOUR—Whole coloured black, red, blue, fawn, cream or white, frequently shaded but not in patches or parti-coloured (underpart of tail and back of thighs frequently of a lighter colour).

SIZE—Dogs 48-56 cm (19-22 ins.) at shoulder. Bitches 46-51 cm (18-20 ins.) at shoulder.

FAULTS—Any departure from the foregoing points should be considered a fault and the seriousness with which the fault should be regarded should be in exact proportion to its degree.

NOTE—Male animals should have two apparently normal testicles descended into the scrotum.

CANADA

The Canadian standard reads basically as the American one used to before it was clarified.

General Appearance—A massive, cobby, powerful dog, active and alert, with strong, muscular development, and perfect balance. Body squares with height of leg at shoulder; head, broad and flat, with short, broad, and deep muzzle, accentuated by a ruff; the whole supported by straight, strong legs. Clothed in a shining, offstanding coat, the Chow is a masterpiece of beauty, dignity, and untouched naturalness.

Head—Large and massive in proportion to size of dog, with broad, flat skull; well filled under the eyes; moderate stop; and proudly carried.

Expression—Essentially dignified, lordly, scowling, discerning, sober, and snobbish—one of independence.

Muzzle—Short in comparison to length of skull; broad from eyes to end of nose, and of equal depth. The lips somewhat full and overhanging.

Teeth—Strong and level, with a scissors bite; should neither be overshot, nor undershot.

Nose—Large, broad, and black in color. *Disqualification*—nose spotted or distinctly other color than black, except in blue Chows, which may have solid blue or slate noses.

Tongue—A blue-black. The tissues of the mouth should approximate black. *Disqualification*—tongue red, pink, or obviously spotted with red or pink.

Eyes—Dark, deep-set, of moderate size, and almond-shaped.

Ears—Small, slightly rounded at tip, stiffly carried. They should be placed wide apart, on top of the skull, and set with a slight, forward tilt. *Disqualification*—drop ear or ears. A drop ear is one which is stiffly carried or stiffly erect, but which breaks over at any point from its base to its tip.

Body—Short, compact, with well-sprung ribs, and let down in the flank.

Neck—Strong, full, set well on the shoulders.

Shoulders—Muscular, slightly sloping.

Chest—Broad, deep, and muscular. A narrow chest is a serious fault.

Back—Short, straight, and strong.

Loins—Broad, deep, and powerful.

Tail—Set well up and carried closely to the back, following line of spine at start.

Forelegs—Perfectly straight, with heavy bone and upright pasterns.

Hind Legs—Straight-hocked, muscular, and heavy-boned.

Feet—Compact, round, catlike, with thick pads.

Gait—Completely individual. Short and stilted because of straight hocks.

Coat—Abundant, dense, straight, and off-standing; rather coarse in texture with a soft, woolly undercoat. It may be any clear color, solid throughout, with lighter shadings on ruff, tail, and breechings.

Disqualifications—Nose spotted or distinctly other than black, except in blue Chows, which may have solid blue or slate noses. Tongue red, pink or obviously spotted with red or pink. Drop ear or ears.

The following is the proposed amendment to the standard that would include the smooth variety of coat:

Coat and Colour—The smooth Chow Chow is judged by the same standard as the rough variety with the exception of coat length. The Smooth should have the same woolly undercoat, harsh texture and dense outer coat as the rough variety, but the Smooth's outer coat is short and gives a sleek appearance. There should be no obvious ruff or feathering on legs and tail.

7

The Illustrated Blueprint
of the Chow Chow

THIS CHAPTER IS BASED on the adage "a picture is worth a thousand words." All illustrations are those of the author. She hopes that the simplicity of line drawings proves helpful to those who wish a visual clarification of the American breed Standard.

There will always be a variety of type within the breed. Some bloodlines will be more exaggerated, others will be plainer. The bottom line to anyone's interpretation, breeder, exhibitor or judge, is that the Chow Chow must be balanced overall and be able to see, breathe, hear, walk and eat. Here, then, is the blueprint to hopefully make all parts of the dog come together for you.

Clothed in a smooth or an offstanding rough double coat, the Chow is a masterpiece of beauty, dignity and naturalness, unique in his blue-black tongue, scowling expression and stilted gait.

The head is large in proportion to the dog (center), not small (left) or so exaggerated as to make the dog seem top heavy (right).

The correct square muzzle.

The muzzle on the left falls away under the eyes and the one on the right is overly padded. Both fail to impart a square impression.

The top skull is broad and flat (left), not domed (right).

The toplines of the muzzle and skull are approximately parallel, joined by a moderate stop.

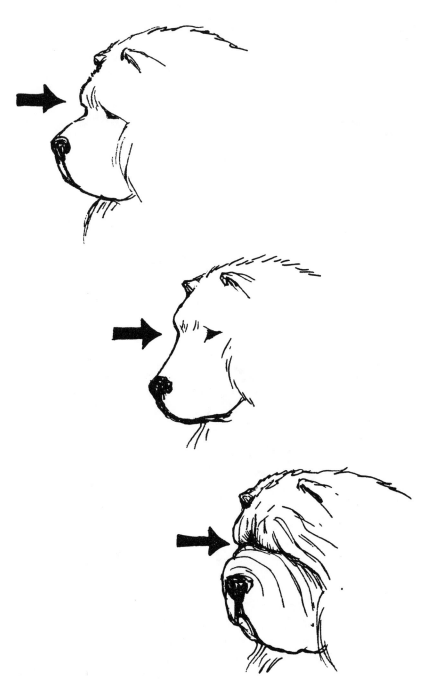

The padding of the brows may make the stop appear steeper than it is. Correct stop (left), too shallow (center) and too deep (right).

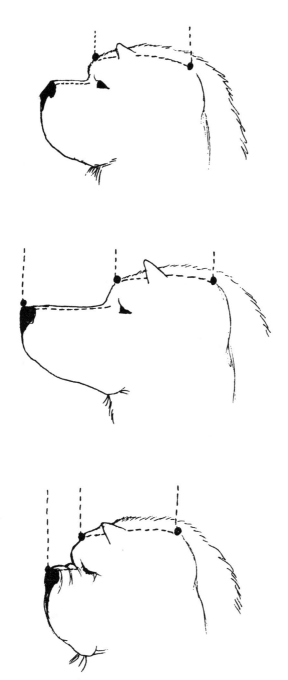

The muzzle is short in comparison to the length of the top skull (top), not equal (center) or less than one-third the head length (bottom).

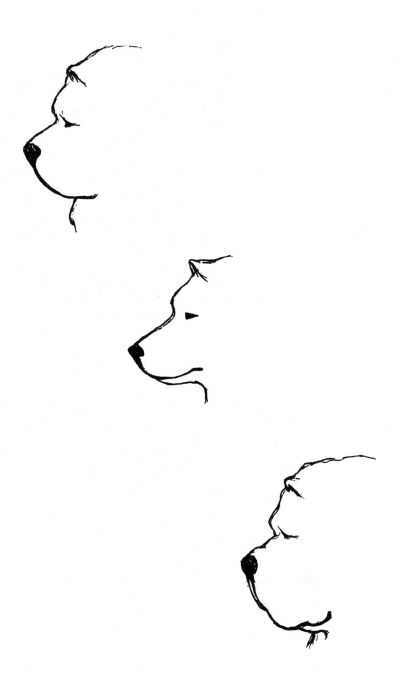

The upper lips should completely cover the lower lips (left), not tightly drawn (center) or pendulous (right).

Disqualifying fault—Nose spotted or distinctly other color than black except in blue Chows which may have solid blue or slate noses. Take note: A true cream Chow will eventually have a disqualifying dudley nose. Judges should therefore check for artificial coloring if the nose on a cream is black.

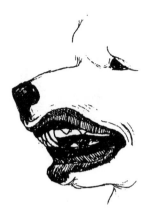

A solid black mouth is ideal.

Disqualifying fault—The top surface or edges of the tongue red or pink or with one or more spots of red or pink. The underside of the tongue is not considered.

Bite should be scissors (left), not overshot (center) or undershot (right).

Eyes placed wide apart and obliquely, of moderate size and almond-shaped (left). Big, round (center) and downturned eyes (right) ruin expression.

The **serious faults** of entropion (left) with the eyelid turning in and ectropion (right) with the eyelid rolling out and drooping.

Serious fault—The pupils wholly or partially obscured by loose skin.

Correct erect ear with a slight forward tilt (left). **Disqualifying faults**—Drop ears: one broken at the base (center) and one broken near the tip (right).

The inner corner of the ear should be on top of the skull and align with the outside corner of the eye (left). Ears set too closely (center) and too low (right).

The Chow's expression is essentially scowling, dignified, lordly, discerning, sober and snobbish.

The neck should carry the head above the topline when standing at attention (left) and not be so short set as to give a stunted look (right).

Body to be short, compact, close coupled, strongly muscled, broad, deep and well let down in the flank (left). Not to be long, rangy, lacking muscle, narrow and with a tuck-up of the underline (right).

179

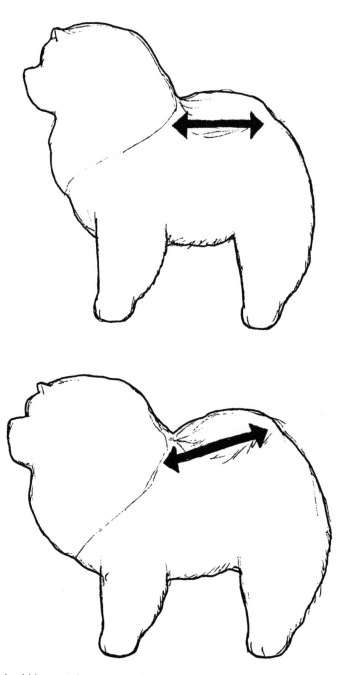

Topline should be straight, strong and level and not jacked-up so as to make the dog appear to be running downhill.

Rear and front bone should be approximately equal (left), not heavier in the front as is all too commonly seen (right).

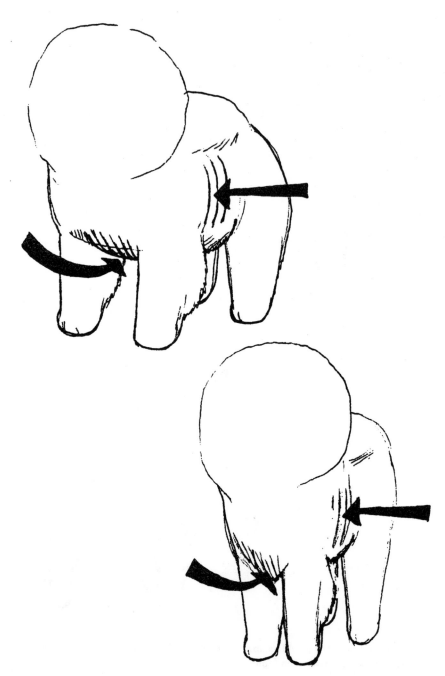

Chest to be broad, deep and muscular (left). **Serious fault**—Narrow or slab-sided chest (right).

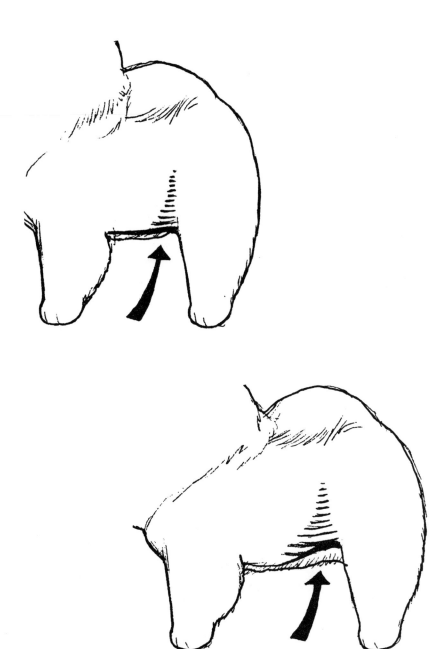

Loin should be short, broad and deep (left), not long, narrow and tucked-up (right).

Powerful rump and thigh muscles give a level croup (left), not a steeper one (right).

(Left to right) An ideal tail, set high and following straight up the spine; good tail, set high and begins to follow spine at its start; incorrect tail, set too low.

(Left to right) Incorrect corkscrew tail; incorrect gay tail and incorrect stub tail.

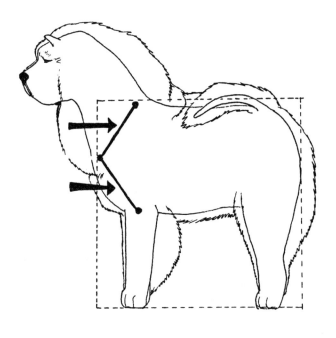

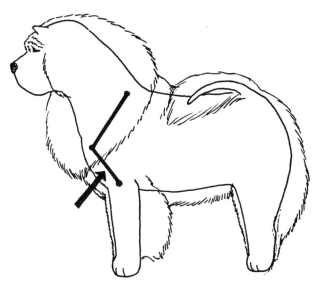

The length of the upper arm should be comparable to the length of the shoulder blade, not shorter.

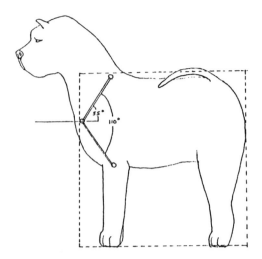

The spine of the shoulder forms an angle of
approximately 55 degrees with the horizontal
line and approximately 110 degrees with the
upper arm.

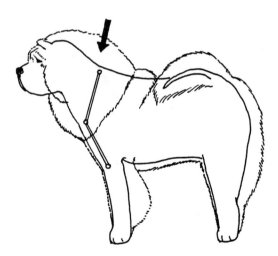

An overly straight shoulder will impede neck
carriage and movement.

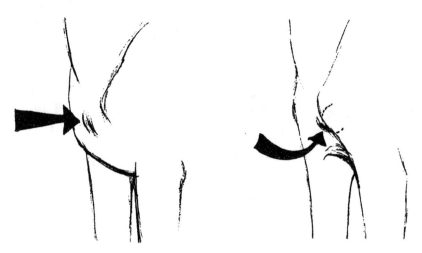

The point of sternum slightly in front of the shoulder points (left) instead of behind (right) which will give a caved-in look.

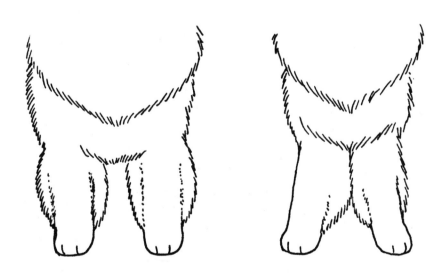

Forelegs pictured in coat, correctly parallel (left) and incorrectly in a tripod (right).

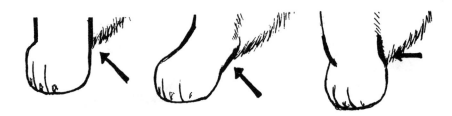

Pasterns to be short and upright (left), not so-called down in the pasterns (center) or knuckled over (right).

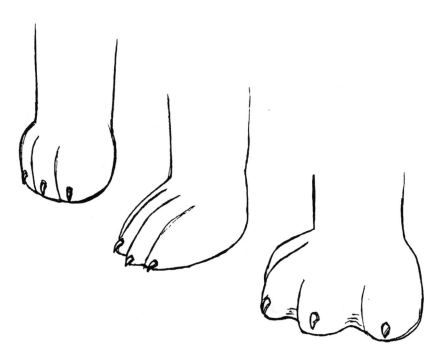

Proper round, cat-like foot (left). Incorrect hare foot (center) and splayed foot (right).

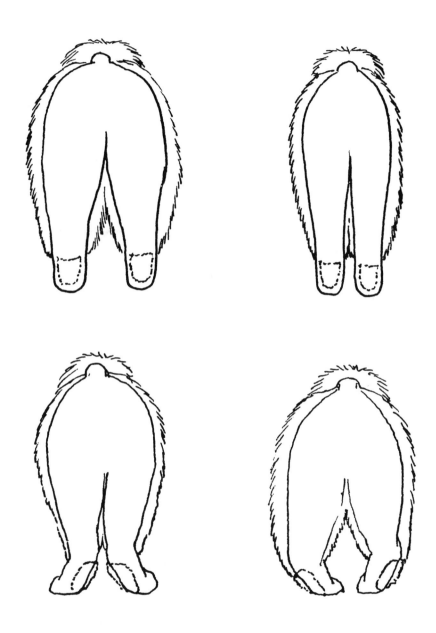

(Left to right). The correct hind legs are straight, parallel and broadly spaced as consistent with a broad pelvis. Incorrect rears include closely-spaced hind legs determined by a narrow pelvis, cow-hocked legs and bowed-out legs.

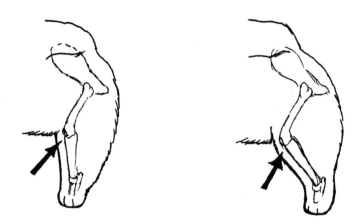

Stifle joint shows little angulation (left). It is not overly angulated (right).

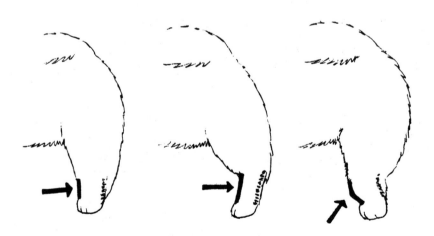

The hock joint should be short (left), not long (center) or have the **serious fault** of bowing forward (right) or to either side. Such a breaking condition is called "double-hocked" in slang.

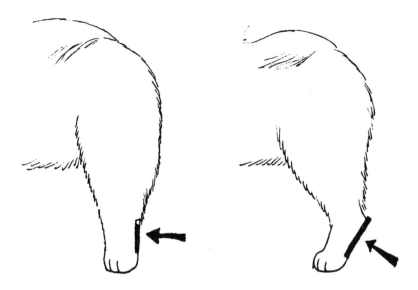

The metatarsals are short and perpendicular to the ground (left), not long and incorrectly angled (right).

Rough coat comes in all lengths. Smooth coat should have no obvious ruff or feathering on the legs or tail.

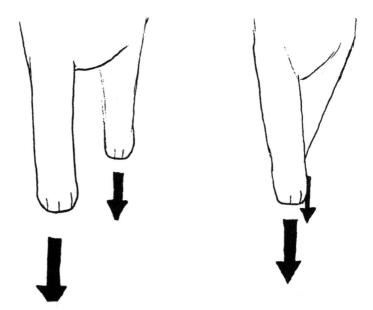

Viewed from the front, the line of bone from shoulder joint to pad remains straight as the dog moves (left), inclining slightly inwardly as the speed increases (right).

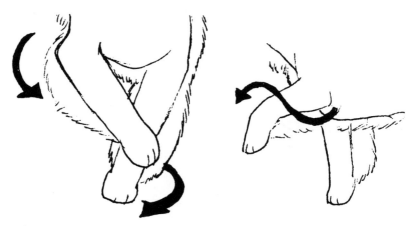

The front legs must not swing out in semi-circles (left) nor mince or show any evidence of hackney action (right).

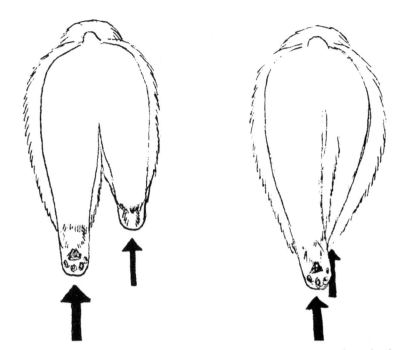

Viewed from the rear, the line of bone from hip joint to pad remains straight as the dog moves (left), inclining slightly inwardly as speed increases (right).

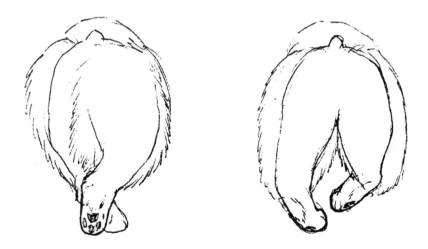

What will happen when the stifle joints incorrectly do not point in the line of travel.

It is from the side that the unique stilted action is most easily assessed. Also note how the shoulder angle determines restricted front reach. The Chow should move with quick, short steps, not long, lumbering strides or high reach in the front or drive in the reach. A Chow's feet will minimally clear the ground because power is transmitted efficiently through the straight hindquarters, short-coupled body and the front assembly of a properly-built Chow.

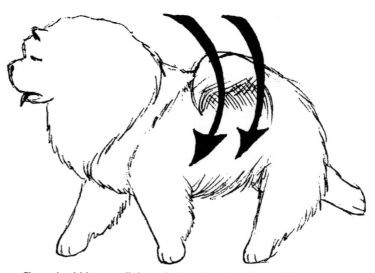

There should be no roll through the midsection when a Chow moves.

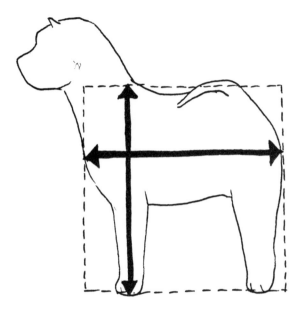

The square profile is determined by measuring from the forechest to the point of the buttocks. This should *equal* the height at the highest point of the withers.

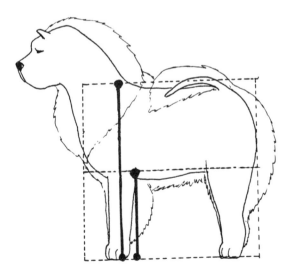

Distance from tip of elbow is half the height at the withers.

Serious faults; a vertical rectangle (left) and a horizontal rectangle (right).

Equally objectionable are snipey, fine-boned specimens and overdone, ponderous, cloddy specimens.

196

Because of its deep-set eyes the Chow has limited peripheral vision and is best approached within the scope of that vision (upper right). Coming from above or behind may startle him, causing him to pull back (left) or swing around (right) to see you.

The average height of adult specimens is 17 to 20 inches at the withers but in every case consideration of overall proportions and type should take precedence over size. If too tall, the Chow will invariably be rangy (left). If too short, the Chow will invariably appear proportionately dwarfed with exaggerated features (right).

There is an impression of femininity in bitches as compared with an impression of masculinity in dogs. However, dependent on the bloodline, one might consider a specimen as a doggy bitch or a bitchy dog as compared to another type of Chow.

8

The Character of
the Chow Chow

HOUSEBREAKING A CHOW, one of the cleanest of breeds, is quite easy. If you give your puppy a strict schedule, you'll be able to fully break him to going outside within a week. If your work schedule or the weather prevents this, resort to paper training. This is almost always an immediate success. Remember, Chowlets whose eyes are not even open will crawl to a remote corner of the whelping box to avoid soiling their sleeping quarters.

Chow Chows are best kenneled separately or, if paired, with the opposite sex. It is a rare but possible situation to run several dogs together. I wouldn't recommend it. Once two dogs have a fight, they will never forget it. They may temporarily forgive, but won't forget. To keep them together will eventually invite trouble.

Chows are adaptable to both city and country living. They can be content living the lounge-lizard life with minimal activity and exercise. They can also be tireless bundles of energy as they patrol their home's acreage. Chows of mine have shared an efficiency apartment in the city during my college days. Their exercise alternated between walks on lead and romps in the run my kindly landlord allowed. Most of my present kennel dogs have spent some time playing house dog and seem to be happy both ways.

Be firm with your Chow from the moment you bring him home. Chows are quite capable of getting the upper hand. A stern voice, not yelling, is enough correction for dealing with this sensitive breed. Hitting your dog is never called for unless he snaps at a person or another animal. In that instance, smack up under his chin with your palm outstretched.

It's a good idea to teach the command of stand, stay to your Chow. If he backs away from a stranger you want him to meet, determine if that person was correctly approaching him from the front. The breed has poor peripheral vision and doesn't necessarily see well from above, beside and behind. The worst thing you can do as your Chow leans into your lap is to reassure him it's okay. It is not okay. Firmly tell him "no," then set him up with the stand, stay command. Praise him properly when he cooperates.

The one-man dog label you will so often hear refers to the fact that a Chow will give undying devotion to the one individual he or she chooses. He or she will tolerate and, yes, be even perfectly friendly towards others. It is incorrect to believe that the Chow will like only one person and attack all others.

A good Chow temperament will accept anyone you will, but can be aloof about it. His or hers is a dignified bearing rather than a fawning clown. However, I encourage outgoing, clown-like behavior in my puppies. As the Chowlets mature, they will usually settle into a more reserved attitude.

Chows are not ones to pick a fight with other breeds. However, if provoked, a Chow will fight to the finish. He or she has one of the strongest jaws of any breed. The Chow's peculiar sweet smell seems, sometimes, to disturb other breeds.

The Chow is unusually adept at remembering things both good and bad. Therefore, try to make his initial puppyhood experiences positive ones. Everything becomes symbolic to your youngster. The car ride home should be pleasant with no injuries or loud, scary noises.

The people he first meets will be interpreted by him on a broad basis. So, try to introduce him to only screened, sensible people in the beginning. In other words, if a very large woman wearing a hat pinches or spooks your puppy, you may find yourself later having to convince him that all heavy set women or people wearing hats aren't out to hurt him. It can be done, but a good first encounter would spare your having to do it.

Therefore, think in prejudiced terms of each person who handles your Chowlet. View the small girl as representing all children; the six foot three inch man will symbolize all tall people; the mailman covers all uniformed people and so forth. Once your pup has many positive experiences, he'll be a well-socialized dog. As is his Chow nature, he may be instinctively suspicious of new faces from then on, but is more apt to give them the benefit of the doubt.

Chows are virtually silent when walking about the house. However, when they decide to bark at a killer leaf, it can be described as a strangled, gargling sound.

Do not ask to buy a Chow Chow for a guard dog, and certainly do not subject this breed to guard dog training. A Chow will instinctively protect his loved ones. Do not encourage aggressive behavior or you may face potential lawsuits.

Years ago, a friend and I were returning from a Boston dog show. She was driving her own car when we became lost in a particularly dangerous district. As the derelicts staggered all around us, I thought "Anise," my mild-mannered bitch, would tear apart the car's interior. She lunged at the windows, baring her teeth. She sensed how frightened my friend was to be in that neighborhood and rose to the occasion. This was the same bitch who used to cross her front legs and serenely accept whatever came her way.

A Chow gives ample opportunity to an intruder to take the hint and back off. His formidable demeanor should be discouraging enough, but, if not, he will follow it up by a barely audible growl. Pushing the defensive dog any further may result in a severe bite.

The obedience people I know have found the Chow to be quick to learn commands, but stubborn at times with executing routines. My first Chow came to me at two years of age. She knew no commands, not even "sit." Within a few months, she had a repertoire of parlor tricks.

I met a couple in a travelling carnival show who had a dog act comprised of Chows and Samoyeds. They were aware of their Chows' inopportune stubborn streak. The dogs might brilliantly perform their tricks for three shows, then sit or trot off the stage during the fourth. The couple chose to accept the audience's laughter and write it off at that.

An idiocyncrasy of the breed is their reluctance to step on

dew-covered grass. A frolic in the ocean surf may not faze them and literally soaking their feet in their water dish may be of their own volition. But, to many Chows, asking them to walk across the damp early morning ground may result in balking and/or bunny-hopping.

9

How to Choose
A Chow Chow

ENTER THE WORLD of Chowdom with a commitment to only do right by the breed. If you simply want a pet quality companion, plan to neuter your Chow. If it's show quality you want, know that the dog show game is a sport that will eat up your time, money and emotions. If it's breeding stock you're after, be assured that breeding will drain your time, money and emotions even more if you do it ethically. Therefore, you should determine whether you want a Chow Chow for a pet, show and/or breeding animal before you begin visiting reputable kennels or private breeders.

A pet differs from the show potential puppies in that it may have a disqualifying fault such as a spotted tongue, dudley nose, drop ears or only one testicle. It might have a serious fault such as entropion or a narrow chest or possess an undershot or overshot bite. It might simply have too plain a head or a bad tailset.

No matter what the fault, it should not be so serious as to be detrimental to the health of your dog. Corrective surgery is possible on a pet, but is against the rules of the American Kennel Club for show competition.

The reputable breeder will grade each Chowlet against the Chow Chow Standard point for point and decide how well it measures up. A pet price may be considerably lower than a show price. With the buyer's agreement, my personal policy is to withhold the blue AKC registration application slip. When the buyer eventually has his or her pet neutered, I refund part of the purchase price and transfer the papers. The bottom line to pet ownership is that you've bought a Chow to be your companion hopefully for twelve or more years. Do not use the animal for breeding purposes, as it will only serve to undermine the betterment of the breed.

In some states it is illegal to sell puppies at less than eight weeks of age. A pet quality puppy could realistically leave for his new home at eight to ten weeks of age.

If you are looking for show and/or breeding stock, the rule is, the older the better. You will have a truer picture of what you are buying. Just be certain it has been properly socialized. A minimum age of ten to twelve weeks is not unreasonable. At these ages you can be sold show potential. It should have no serious faults according to the standard and certainly no disqualifying ones.

Problems such as the possible development of hip dysplasia, entropion, bad bites and so forth should be discussed with the breeder. Any guarantees should be written, not just verbal. A breeder can't guarantee whether or not any serious conditions will develop. However, he or she can guarantee what, if anything, he or she will do should something go seriously wrong. You will most likely be required to neuter the afflicted animal before any refund or replacement will be made.

Chows are experiencing a wave of popularity. There are staggering numbers of them, but the quality is proportionately poor. Therefore, find an established breeder who will refer you elsewhere if he or she has nothing for you.

It is better to buy your dog or bitch outright with no strings attached. Do not accept a special price with a complicated puppies-back deal. However, if you are offered an opportunity to obtain a proven valuable Chow with conditions of sale attached, you might consider it. Perhaps it is an established breeder who must cut back on the number of dogs in his or her kennel. A co-ownership in this case allows you a headstart with quality and experience and enables the breeder to continue his or her bloodline.

If you are looking for a show potential pup, you should attend dog shows, especially regional and National Specialty shows. There

Hopefully, your Chow will be your companion for twelve or more years. Am. Can. Ch. Teabear's Thyme Will Tell, almost fifteen years of age, and her great-great-great grandson, Teabear's Thyme Immemorial, pictured at ten weeks of age. *Kip*

Red Chow puppies may have black masks when young, but they usually fade to clear red or cream when older. Cinnamons' charcoal grey masks usually fade to pinkish-silver when they reach adulthood. *Kip*

Plan so that your new Chowlet comes home during a period when you can spend lots of time with him or her. The holidays are too hectic. Therefore, a photo such as this could be provided by the breeder to tide you over until a quieter time when the puppy should join you. *Kip*

you will form an idea of what appeals to you and/or what is correct. Next, visit kennels known for that type and study magazines before and after the visits. Certainly meet the dam of the litter. View the rest of the dogs in the pedigree either in the flesh or through pictures.

Chow type can be quite diverse. In spite of what the Standard says, you will find a range in type of Chows from those resembling Finnish Spitz to those who look like coated Shar-Pei. You want the happy medium, an unmistakable Chow Chow.

If you have decided on a show potential puppy, your best bet is to find a good red bitch. Red is a good color choice for relative success in the ring and in a breeding program. A female versus a male allows you far more flexibility when choosing a future mate. A black female would be a wise alternative. Avoid getting involved with dilute color breeding at first. Also, blues and cinnamons may have their pigmentation fade at an age you might want to be showing them. To buy a cream Chow puppy for show is a lesson in futility. Even if it has a black nose early on, a true cream's nose will fade to a dudley disqualification later on.

The color of puppy coat on a Chow will most likely not be the same shade as the adult guard hairs and undercoat. Even puppy coat black is duller than its adult counterpart. Look on the muzzle, the feet and above the eyes for a hint of the true color to be.

Red puppy coat, to the novice, is mistakenly called tan, buff, champagne or brown. Black may have a blue-black or brown-black cast, and may have silver hair in the tail and breechings. A blue puppy will usually be the color of a blue Persian kitten and may have silver in the tail, breechings and muzzle. Cinnamon puppy coat ranges from a greyish-pink to a pinkish-sand color. Creams will be creamy-white when young, but develop biscuit discoloration on the ears, saddle and sometimes muzzle and legs.

Chow Chow puppies grow extremely rapidly. Their weight and size should at least double in the first week of life. As soon as their eyes open, around ten to fourteen days, they become endearing teddy bear look-alikes. This, unfortunately, makes them all appealing whether they're of good, mediocre or bad quality. Therefore, be sure to look closely.

I find the most telling ages to look at Chows are at birth, at six weeks, ten weeks, four months, eighteen months and three to four years.

The newborn pup shows skeletal proportions. To a trained eye, lengths, widths, angles and thicknesses can be imagined on an

Six-week-old female. Plusses: lovely neck carriage and length; high tailset; short back and good shoulders. Faults: snipey muzzle, light bone and thin pads.

Kip

Six-week-old male. Plusses: excellent headpiece, with broad muzzle and skull and appropriately-sized and placed ears; heavy bone front and rear; deep body; perfect tailset, high and following straight up the spine and good neck carriage. Faults: short upper arm and curled toes with thin pads.　　　*Kip*

Ten-week-old male. Plusses: lovely muzzle and broad top skull; heavy bone; thick pads and tight feet. Faults: large, low set, drop ears (shaved, they eventually went up) and light eye.

Feresten

Ten-week-old female. Plusses: short, compact body; straight legs of moderate bone; tight feet; hard coat; clean eyes and high tailset. Faults: lack of fill under the eyes and large ears. *Feresten*

enlarged scale. For some reason, the thicker the base of the tail, the heavier the leg bone of the dog will be. Again, it's a trained eye to be able to discern what constitutes "thick." Obviously, how the bite will come in, if the tail will tightly go up, if ears will stand and how the dog will move, are unknowns at this point.

At five to six weeks of age the temperament is forming. The pups are weaned and are now looking to humans for contact and food. The breeder may administer actual temperament tests to grade who is submissive, dominant, obstinate, aggressive, obedient or shy in the litter. Or, years of experience can properly interpret puppies' attitudes and aptitudes for placement. The most gorgeous specimen in the world with an aggressive or a cowering temperament won't do. Temperament is of the utmost importance whether your Chow serves in a show, breeding or pet capacity.

At six weeks of age, the puppy teeth are in, blue-black pigment should have fully covered the tongue, tails are up and ears may or may not be up. Legs may appear too short and/or angulated at this age. Feet should be tight and pads should be thick, not paper thin. Testicles on males may not be fully descended, but should be able to be located. This is a good age for the breeder to have the litter's first inoculation, worming and veterinary examination.

Ten weeks of age seems to give a good idea of future proportions. Skull, muzzle, shoulder angle, length and level of back, length of leg, neck carriage, feet and tailset can be evaluated fairly accurately. Allowing for the fact that muscle tone is developing, movement is pretty much on target. In most cases, testicles should be fully descended. Eyes should indicate if they will be clean or suffer from entropion, ectropion or blocked tear ducts. Normal tearing from dusty puppy play or urine's ammonia fumes will be a slight, clear discharge from the inner or outer corner of the eye. Be leery of heavy discharge which may be indicative of infection, irritation or ill health. Look closely to see if the eyelashes are rubbing up against the eyeball. Or observe if the lower lids droop away from the eye. These are entropic and ectropic conditions, respectively. Personality is apparent, but is young enough for you to correct if there is a problem.

Four months of age is the same as above except that the Chowlet is moving more confidently. You can therefore evaluate front and rear movement more accurately. If you wait until six months of age, your Chow should have been fully vaccinated, totally socialized and lead broken by his breeder. Expect to pay more for the breeder's time and energy at this point.

At eighteen months of age, adolescence is concluding and the Chow has reached his adult height. He has probably completely blown his puppy coat and is in semi-passable adult coat. It will usually take two complete sheddings of adult coat to reach the mature bloom.

In slow-maturing bloodlines, Chow dogs and bitches will begin to come into their own between three and four years of age. This means the headpiece, coat, muscle tone and attitude aren't fully developed before then. It's a worthwhile test of patience though, because Chows who develop too early often break down or become too coarse.

With meticulous care, such as that given to Specialty winner Ch. Dusten's Anticipation, you may enjoy your Chow Chow's loving companionship for many rewarding years.

10

Special Care of a Chow Chow

CHOWS ARE, FOR THE MOST PART, a hardy lot. Their coat, although difficult to keep up during puppyhood, is a double one and fairly easy to maintain in adulthood.

Unless they are of bloodlines throwing ear problems, your Chow's ears will go up by themselves. If by eight weeks of age they are not up, it will help to round off the tips of hair with thinning shears. If by ten weeks they are still not up, you might try shaving them and bracing them up and towards each other. Seek professional instruction with this or you may permanently crease the ears. Sometimes your Chow's ears will drop during the teething stage, but will return erect on their own.

The pink tongue with which your Chow was born should fill in completely blue-black on its own. Many breeders supplement with kelp to add iodine to the diet. However, all the kelp in the world will not correct poor hereditary pigmentation.

Pay careful attention to your Chow's eyes. Any irritations that cause him to rub or squint his eyes may cause hysterical entropion. This is a vicious cycle of rubbing that creates swelling, which in turn forces the eyelids to turn in. This entropic condition leads to more rubbing. Left untreated, it may cause permanent damage to the eyeball. Use warm, not hot, water on a terry facecloth to gently wipe matter away from the eyes. Ask your veterinarian for a topical ointment or solution that you can routinely use if dust or pollen in the eyes is a problem.

Proper catlike Chow feet may keep the nails short by walking on rough surfaces. Use nail trimmers if you find they aren't being worn down. Some Chows are prone to interdigital cysts. I once heard of a rare situation where the pads lifted, thereby inviting fungal infection.

Chows grow rapidly, although some lines are slow maturers. It's best to keep your dog on the light side, weight-wise, so as not to cause undue strain on pasterns, hips, back, etc. As much as cute Chow puppies can and do often win in the ring, it's not worth pushing your pup's growth too fast.

Never drop your Chow. Be in the habit of making sure all four paws are on the ground before letting go. Remember that you are dealing with a straight stifle, not an angulated breed. Picture, if you will, jumping from a garage roof and not flexing your knees when you land.

Ordinarily, Chows are not climbers, diggers or jumpers when it comes to fencing that will contain them. A four-foot high fence will usually suffice. I use six-foot high chain link. This is more to keep neighborhood dogs out, rather than to keep my Chows in. Dirt runs are the best for developing Chow feet, but the mud and parasite factors should be considered. I've found one-inch crushed stone is best. Pea stone, however, is the favored surface by most Chowists I know. Other than for hygiene, the worst surface would be concrete. It's too much shock absorption for straight legs to pound on. It also breaks coat.

Many blue and black Chows tend to sunburn or develop tones of red in their coats if left exposed to too much sun. Other than using commercial coat sunscreens, you should keep them kenneled in shade and exercised at night.

Although some Chows will choose to lie in the full sun for hours, you must provide cool shade as relief from the heat and humidity. It's best to keep several blue ice packs in your freezer all year long. Overheating or heat prostration necessitates soaking your Chow in cold water to bring down the temperature. Blue ice packs will help cool the water and can also be pressed up against the abdomen, groin and head.

The best way to travel or ship your dog in warm weather is on a specially constructed crate cooler. It's built to fit your dog's crate and because of its insulating properties will stay cold for many hours. This is critical when shipping and risking layovers. Some Chow fanciers fashion a cool surface by using a crate's inverted metal tray over blue ice packs, but it doesn't stay cold as long as the crate cooler.

A glistening coat in full bloom adds to the characteristic alert appearance of B.I.S. winner Can. Am. Ch. Mi Pao's Timang.

11

How to Groom
the Chow Chow

Initial Training

The Chowlet you bring home should be taught to quietly lie on its side for grooming. A grooming table is a must for an exhibitor. A non-skid bath mat on a sturdy card table will suffice for the pet owner.

To teach your puppy this, wrap your arms around him as one would carry a lamb. (See illustration.) Gently turning him over on his side and slightly leaning on him, reassure him. The first few times you do this, simply rub your hands over him rather than doing any heavy-duty grooming.

The wooly puppy coat is best tackled with a poodle comb, a three-inch deep one with widely-spaced teeth. A one-inch comb with teeth spaced both closely and far apart will be used behind the ears and on the metatarasals. Brush, not comb, adult coat.

With the puppy lying on his side, start at the top of the shoulders and work your way back toward the rear. Hold the hair back with one hand and comb out a small amount of hair forward. (See illustration.) Use short deep strokes. Make sure you are combing down to the skin. If you comb over only the top surface,

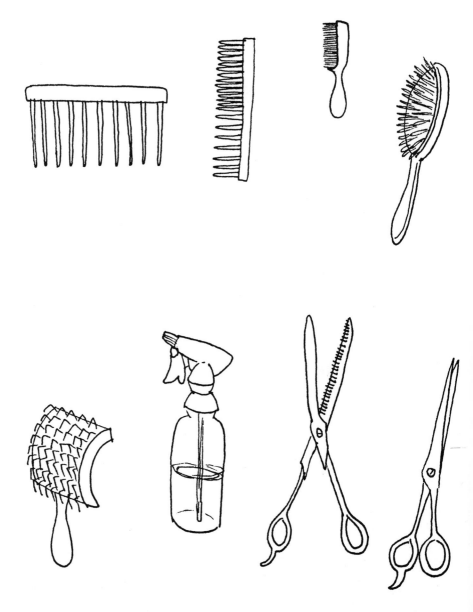

Grooming equipment that will cover the various stages of Chow coat: top row (left to right) three-inch deep poodle comb, one-and-a-half-inch comb, widely spaced at one end and narrowly spaced at the other, flea comb, curved pin brush with metal rounded tips or natural bristles; bottom row (left to right) slicker brush, spray bottle for misting, thinning shears with one or both edges serrated and barber shears.

With your arms wrapped around him, gently turn your puppy over on his side onto the grooming table.

Push coat with your non-grooming hand in the opposite direction to which you are brushing or combing. Here, pushing toward the rear, brushing the coat forward, from the skin out.

you'll tend to card the coat. This will virtually create one big mat on your pup. As you finish combing out each section you're holding, keep moving toward the rear of the dog. Finish the midsection.

Move to the hind leg. Comb it in a downward direction. Do the front leg in a downward direction. Comb the top and side of the mane. Turn the puppy over and repeat.

Sit your Chow up. Work up from between the front legs, pushing up with one hand and combing down. When you get to the mane, comb down and out.

Stand the dog up and work up from the back of the hind foot. Comb the metatarsal hair straight back. Push the breechings up on an angle towards the anus; comb down and out. Pretend the wind is blowing from the rear and fanning the hind end. Starting behind the front foot, hold the coat up. Comb down and back.

Hold the tail straight up and work up from its base. Comb it down all around. (See illustration.) Lay tail back in place and fan all the hair forward.

Scissoring

Shape all four feet. Put the blade of the thinning shears under the excess hair and lift up. Snip and lift. Snip and lift. Cut across the front of the foot. Do not indent around each toe. (See illustration.) Do, however, pick foot up and remove excess hair from around pads from underneath.

Use the one-inch comb on the metatarsal hair. Comb out and back again. Point thinning shears straight down if you find it easier to do this with your Chow standing. Otherwise, support the leg backwards and scissor with the thinning shears pointing up. Let your puppy return to standing every once in a while to review the progress of your handiwork. Take it a little bit at a time. You do not want to take the hair off all the way down to the skin. Instead, try to leave enough on to make the front and rear bone appear equal. Leaving too much on will ruin the straight-hocked appearance. (See illustration.)

Bathing

A pet Chow rarely requires a bath. His coat and skin are naturally sweet-smelling and flea-resistant. Too much bathing will dry out these properties. Semi-weekly brushing will usually keep

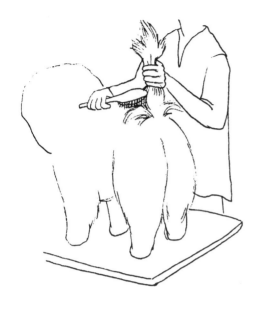

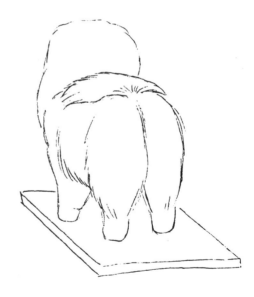

Hold the tail straight up and work up from its base. Brush it down all round (left). When you reach the tip, lay the tail back in place and fan all the hair forward (right).

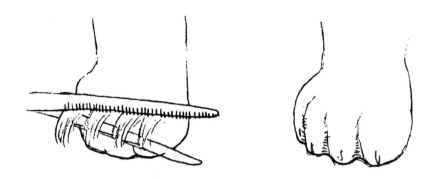

Round off the foot with scissors and thinning shears (left). Do not indent around each toe (right).

Leave enough hair on the metatarsals to make the front and rear bone appear equal (left). It will look unbalanced if you take too much off (center) and too unkempt if you don't take enough off (right).

your dog in fine shape. A hot bath will loosen the coat that is ready to shed out once a year.

A show Chow requires more frequent bathing, whether it be full or spot bathing. The dirt of the dog show sites and the grit that clings to coat conditioners make it so.

Thoroughly brush out your dog. Carefully split and comb out any mats. Put a few drops of mineral oil or ear medication in his ears and plug them with several cotton balls each. You can apply an ointment in the eyes, if you'll be using a harsh shampoo.

Soak the coat with warm, not hot, water. Lather, then rinse well. Lather again, then rinse thoroughly. A trick that will help you deep lather through the Chow's double coat is to use a terry facecloth to rub in the shampoo. Apply conditioner, let soak in and rinse out if necessary. Cut the softened nails when you take the dog out of the tub.

Let him shake while you continue using several Turkish towels to blot him. A correct texture of coat will start drying quite rapidly. Unfortunately, the undercoat retains moisture. You must, therefore, concern yourself with drying it thoroughly. Pay particular attention to the underside of the tail and the area it covers. The same care should be taken behind the ears, the elbows and around a male's testicles. Even when you think you've sufficiently dried these areas, some unobtrusive cornstarch or medicated powder won't hurt.

Blow dry the Chow as shown in the diagrams. Use a high-velocity cool heat to blow as you brush. Wait overnight for the coat to settle before you neaten your dog up.

Removal of Whiskers

The removal of whiskers is subject to debate. It's allowable, but some fanciers feel that you are injuring a sensory organ when you do so. You must decide one way or the other, the clean look or the whiskered look. Do not leave the stubble look or feel. If you do remove whiskers, insert your finger inside the lip and push out where you want to cut them. Use the tip of scissors to snip as closely to the skin as possible.

Grooming the Headpiece

Use a flea comb to comb the dead hair off the muzzle. It is also valuable under the bottom jaw and around the lips where food may be trapped. Use the one-inch comb on the skull to comb down and define the scowl. Comb the fine hair behind the ears. Brush the offstanding mane to frame the head. Keep your Chow's bib dry with the dryer or some cornstarch or powder. Secure a towel or bib tightly under the chin until judging.

Trimming

The Chow Chow Standard reads "Obvious trimming or shaping is undesirable." The key word here is *obvious*. A red puppy coat that has been scissored back to expose charcoal grey or black undercoat looks awful. So does a male's underside that has been scalped so much as to leave his penis in plain view. Cutting the mane into a perfect circle is unnatural. Why people scissor-in a tuck-up on a breed that frowns on one is a mystery.

However, do not kid yourself that trimming doesn't exist. Look at most of the top-winning Chows and notice how neat they look. Scissoring, plucking and thinning helped create that look.

Pointy tips on the ears can be rounded off. A low tailset can be made to appear higher, as can a good tailset. A mane hanging in a point and obstructing the front gives an optical illusion of a narrower front. The same holds true for excess coat between the front legs. It's better to lop off long wisps than to try and save them. Scissoring back actually gives a fuller look.

Clipping

Do not think that clipping your Chow down for summer will cool him. Instead, his coat acts as insulation. Even if you've neglected your dog's coat, it is still preferable to carefully comb it out rather than shave it off.

Hot Spots

Moist eczema, or more simply, a hot spot, is the condition whereby your dog will chew on his skin and coat until it becomes a raw, oozing sore. Any number of factors can contribute to your Chow gnawing on himself. Boredom, change in diet, stress, and allergies are usually the cause. Allergies can involve your Chow being overly sensitive to a flea bite. You may not find any fleas on your dog because his skin naturally repels them, but one may eat and run. Some Chows have been found to be allergic to wheat. Therefore, when a corn-based kibble is substituted, an improvement

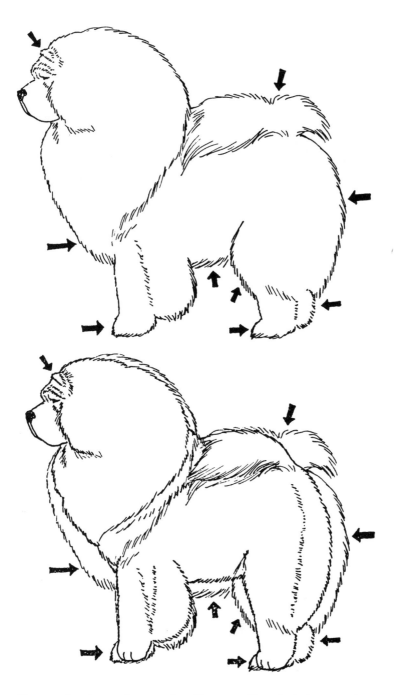

The overabundance of coat makes this square Chow look dumpy and unbalanced. Any neatening up that you might do need not be as drastic as illustrated, but these are key areas that often appear to be "overgrown."

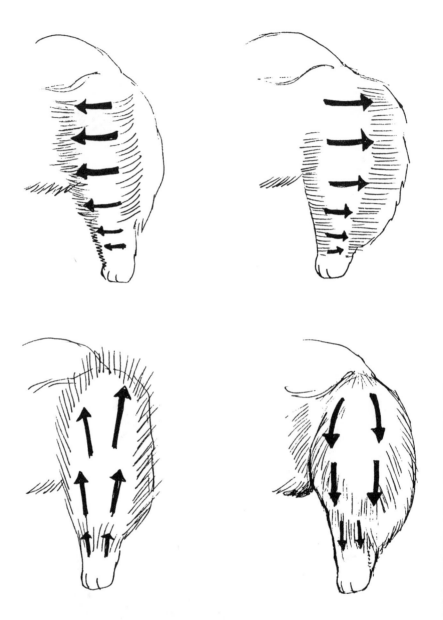

For the fullest possible effect, groom each coat section *in four directions*. For instance, the final direction in which the hind leg should be brushed is down. First brush the whole leg forward (top left), next backward (top right), then up (bottom left) and finally down. Of course, lightly mist with plain water or commercial coat preparations as you groom. The result will be bouffant, with every hair offstanding.

is possible. Basically, if you suspect your dog is having an allergic reaction to something, have your veterinarian conduct a series of tests.

If you can nip a hot spot before it becomes too deep or too infected, you might try something as simple as a cornstarch, not talc-based, medicated powder. The object is to dry up the moisture and relieve your Chow of the itchiness.

If the hot spot is severe, your only recourse is to clip down that area, consult your vet for medicated shampoo and salve, and keep the spot clear of flies. This is a gross subject, but double coats trap moist eczema and invite flies who lay eggs. In a matter of *hours* eggs can become maggots that burrow into the skin. Therefore, treat any hot spot immediately and you should be able to clear it up rather quickly.

Ch. Fa-Ci Yucca by Ch. Fa-Ci Tamarack x Ch. Fa-Ci
Cineraria. Breeder, Jim Facciolli; owner, Carole Whitlock.

Ashbey

12

How to Show a Chow Chow

Y OU WILL DETERMINE the type of collar for your dog depending on the control you need. If a choke collar is called for, make sure it's a jewel-link one. The regular link metal chokes will ruin the mane. A nylon choke often gets entangled in the mane and won't release. A rolled leather choke is an alternative for a dog who's more trained. A martingale collar, or collar and lead combination, is sometimes viable, but usually not with puppy coat. For a dog who needs mild control, a slip lead will do, as will a thin, rolled leather collar and lead.

Part the coat to the skin all around the neck and put the collar in place. If you simply overlap the coat, you'll create an unsightly break in the Chow's outline. A collar high up on the neck will give you the utmost control, but placement directly behind the ears will give your dog a terrible expression. Always be able to pull up at least some mane from how you set the collar.

Some dogs are baited with food or toys and stand on a loose lead. This is fine training for a dog with a lovely, short-backed silhouette. However, it's rarely flattering to the headpiece, especially

The most flattering view of a well-built Chow is the three-quarter angle to show off most of the dog at once. Kneeling beside your dog might bolster confidence.

if the handler has the Chow looking up at him or her. The head should face straight ahead or slightly down depending on the scowl desired.

The most common and flattering pose for a Chow is the three-quarter view. The head, front, four legs, tailset and part of the body and back are visible to the judge. Standing beside your Chow, you might bury your left hand in the mane as you pull it up to help frame the face. Or, you may stand behind your dog while holding the other end of the lead.

Half-kneeling beside or in front of your dog is suitable for a puppy or an inexperienced dog who might appreciate your being down on his level.

Always make sure the judge's approach is within your Chow's limited peripheral vision. Turn your Chow's head slightly toward the judge if he or she incorrectly walks up from behind or beside your dog.

Train your Chow not only to show his teeth, but to open his mouth fully so a judge may explore his tongue. He will be checked not only for his bite as all breeds are, but also for a spotted tongue.

Some handlers and show photographers have the misconception that a Chow's hind legs should be stretched out behind him. The correct position is for you to visualize a vertical straight line from the base of the tail down through the hind foot.

The Chow Chow is not meant to be raced around a ring. He should maintain a steady trot at all times. Even at the group level, either stay with the pace of the Bulldog, Frenchie and Schipperke or let your Chow travel a smaller pattern.

Keep in mind the disqualifications for the breed and check your show specimen before each show. You know he has a solid nose, but that fence fight last night took out a small chunk. Your pleading honorable injury won't suffice; the judge will disqualify if there is any red or pink on the nose. Your Chow's earset is terrific, right? Well, during the bath you got water in his ears which irritated the ear canal. Now, after rubbing his head all night, your dog is holding his ears at odd angles. The solid blue tongue on your male who licked the bowl of frozen water in the dead of winter now has a spot of pink. Your bitch, also with excellent pigment, came into heat and her tongue has faded to shades of pinkish lavender.

In all the above situations, along with routinely checking males for two normally-descended testicles, it's best to lose some entry fees rather than risk disqualification. All of the above mishaps should return to normal in time.

Ch. Marian's Imperial Pandy Bear and owner-trainer John Reigle brighten the lives of two youngsters at the Elizabethtown (PA) Hospital and Rehabilitation Center for Youth. A harness maker custom fit a carting harness for Pandy, ensuring maximum efficiency.

13

The Useful Chow Chow

As MENTIONED in an earlier chapter, Chows have served in hunting, herding, pulling and guarding capacities over the centuries. These instincts are potentially still within the breed. Most Chows today are thought of and kept as quiet showpieces. However, with perseverance in training, their age-old traits can most probably be brought out again. If soundness has not suffered for type, the physical capabilities will also still be there.

The Chow as a model has entered the world of advertising on television, magazines and newspapers. As eye-catching a breed as the Chow is, the consumer is immediately drawn to the ad by his presence.

Then again, if your model is naked by virtue of having shed out his coat, save the wool and take it to spinner. It will make warm yarn that has the feel of angora. Knit or crochet it into a hat, scarf or shawl. Brush out a kennel of Chows and you'll have a whole winter wardrobe!

Mastering the challenge of advanced obedience work yields great satisfaction for both dog and handler, as Shawn clears the BROAD JUMP.

14

The Chow Chow in Obedience

WITH AN INORDINATELY-HIGH pet population of Chows now on the scene, more owners than ever have taken to successfully obedience training their Chows. Basic obedience commands such as sit, stay, down, come and stand, stay provide good manners for any dog.

There are five AKC obedience degrees or titles your Chow may earn: *Companion Dog (C.D.)* which is the *Novice* level and includes: heeling on and off lead, stand for examination, recall (come when called) as well as the long sit and long down (periods of time when your Chow stays put unsupervised); *Companion Dog Excellent (C.D.X.)* in which your Chow will do the more difficult *Open* work and heel free, drop (go flat down) on recall, retrieve (a dumbbell) on the flat (ground or floor), retrieve (a dumbbell) over the high jump, jump a broad jump and wait for you on a long sit and long down; *Utility Dog (U.D.)* where the *Utility* exercises involve giving your Chow hand signals to come, drop, sit, come and finish (sit beside you in the heel position), scent discrimination tests, directed retrieve and as well as directed group stand for examination; *Tracking Dog (T.D.)* or *Tracking Dog Excellent (T.D.X.)* just that.

Shawn walks close to Debbie's left side in HEEL FREE, a Novice or Open exercise.

Shawn sits straight and promptly on order from the judge to HALT in HEEL FREE, a Novice or Open exercise.

For all titles except tracking, a dog must pass all exercises in each series to earn an overall passing score. If he then accumulates a total of at least 170 points out of a possible perfect score of 200, he will have earned a "*leg*" toward his title. By earning three legs, he will capture the obedience title that can follow his registered name for the rest of his days. To earn a Tracking Dog or a Tracking Dog Excellent title, the dog must successfully follow a human scent from the beginning to the end of a track (pattern) set down several hours before the test. The dog must pass only one such official test to earn each of the titles mentioned above.

After a Chow does earn a C.D., he or she might not train for more advanced degrees. This is due, in part, to the jumping requirements being unusually stressful in Chow structure. In 1987, an ongoing concerted effort culminated in petitioning The American Kennel Club to lower the jumping height requirements for Chow Chows.

Even with the obedience requirements as they have always been, the following statistics show us the obedient stars of recent years. They are based on the Chow Chow Club, Inc.'s annual statistician's committee reports.

In 1979, thirteen Chows earned C.D. titles: Da Gung Dzu, owned by Jack Freeman; Sally's Dolly, Robert Dean and Sally Jean Smith; Bobby's Buster, Robert Dean and Sally Jean Smith; Gentleman Joseph Rae-Al, Sharon L. and David L. Shuemake; Starcrest Kodiak, Burton and Kim Lindemoen; Wanda's Fu Lin, Wanda J. Vincent; Bonniebill's Black Bear, William L. Kelley, Jr. and Bonnie Kelley; Carr's Hunter of Lenox, Carroll W. Carr; Genghis Chan Kong, Doyle K. Caldwell; Bernard Duke of Hampton, Jay Mitchell; Sassy's Wind Shi, Jerry and Glenda Dockter; Cinnamon Candy, Karen Pfeifer and Lallipup's Legend of Lorraine, Kim and Burt Lindemoen.

That year, Lallipup's Running Bare, owned by Kim and Burt Lindemoen and Applewood's Ximena, owned by Margot F. Woods, earned their C.D.X. titles.

In 1980, these fifteen Chows added C.D. to their names: Brandy's Copper Wine, owned by Kenneth W. Riddle and Karen L. Stark; Chew's King Bonapart, Kenneth Allen Chew; Mei Chau Poock Gher, Loren Steven Hart and Janet S. Klusmeier Hart; Kamara Rickey's Superboy, Steven R. Kafrissen, MD and Marcia R. Kafrissen; Tokin, Frank A. DeNap and Lavada J. DeNap; Ch. Sal Mae's Smart Alec, Nancy M. and Lewis Cuccia; Caralott La Di

Shawn retrieves the dumbbell in RETRIEVE on the FLAT, an Open exercise.

Gypsy immediately drops to the DOWN position when Debbie gives the verbal command in DROP on RECALL, an Open exercise.

Shawn returns briskly with the dumbbell in RETRIEVE on the FLAT, an Open exercise.

Shawn clears the BROAD JUMP, an Open exercise.

Ling, Carol and Scott Bridgeman; Taro's Oso Negro, Sandra Lee Glew; Princess Tanta, Anthony and Tatiana Schisler; Ro-Jean's Ming Ha Ling, Debbie Hansard; Ebony's Proud Lady, Shirley A. Skelton; Chinabear Merri-Gold, William V. and Janna L. Kohler; Fidler's Azhrarnof Aplwoods, Margot Woods; Hookah, Karen Erickson and Kim Chang's Ping, Fred A. and Victoria H. Settle.

Sandra A. and Robert E. Powell's Pandee's Benjamin Blue was the only one to earn a Companion Dog Excellent title that year.

In 1981, fourteen Chows earned their C.D.: Al De Bear Kuuipo Ua Lani, owned by Mary L. Jones; Biloowan Baby Bear, Kathi and Dennis Munyon; Criskoken Andora, Margaret Crisson; Dandy Bear, Cynthia Thompson; Dychow's Pattimac's Ni Hao, Patricia MacDonald; GR-OWL's Elfin Magic, G. Rivera, Owen Leverich and Annette Crabdree; GR-OWL's Messiah, Tim and Annette Crabdee; Little Geisha, Polly S. Miller and Carl E. Miller, Jr.; Pandee's Blu Sampan, John D. Byrum and Billy Rivera; Patti's Precious Sable Pup, Patricia A. Lane; Roddie's T'ung Hsiung Nikki, J. Cody and Myra and Marci Milligan; Sunrunner Chin Chin, Mrs. B. Stephens; Tian Tian Greta, Judith P. and Anthony Mijares and Tien Ching Lady Nimshi, Sandra Glew. No dog qualified for a C.D.X.

In 1982, the Chows earning their C.D. degree jumped to twenty-nine: Admar's The Dragon Lady, Cecillia Reeder; Black Hawk II, Suzanne Reid; Ch. Cabaret Crackerjack, Jamie and Joan Richard; Caldwell's Honey of Tag-El, Doyle K. Caldwell; Carolyn's Cinnamon Bear, Carolyn Scott; Chee Chee Fu Kwon, James C. and Lynn M. Morgan; Chew's Sasha Ling, Kenneth A. and Vicki L. Chew; Ciao Ciao Buddha, Helen J. and Albert Nickerson; Coronet's Country Boy, Cynthia and Mike Waid; Criskoken Aquarius, Carol M. Mooney; Jim Dandy's Teddy Bear, James W. Ingerham; Joe Lin, Mary D. Weakly; Kentucky Bourbon Red, James P. Waddle; Kuvoi Kin Pooh Bear, Nancy J. Bessette; Laurel Creek's Ginger Lady, Carolyn J. Dyer; Laurel Creek's Mitzsue Bear, Peggy Dotson; Man-Kou Jung Tsay Meng, Camille Gagnon; Matthew's Momma Mei, Emmon M. Storrs; Meenmy Shadow, Victor Cardona and Patricia A. Lane; Meschech Kai Shek, Archie and Debbie Embler; Mi Kimlee, Darlene T. Woods; Ng Ka Py, Catherine and Edmund Halley; Pocono's Chin-Chu-Ling, Nancy Roeber; Richard's Chelsea Belladonna, Richard A. and Trina R. Marostica; Suki-Tai, Karen E. Kebbell; Tasha Rosanna Pride, Rebecca and Gary Lampkin; Ch. Venus Ruby Red Dress, Mickey Stephens; Wild Honey's Pooh

Gypsy, Shawn and Sophie remain on the LONG SIT in a group exercise, Novice or Open work.

Gypsy, Shawn and Sophie remain on the LONG DOWN in a group exercise, Novice or Open work.

Sophie clears the solid jump in DIRECTED JUMPING, a Utility exercise.

Sophie clears the Bar Jump in DIRECTED JUMPING, a Utility exercise.

Bear, Shirley A. Skelton and Wu Li's Peking Prince, James L. and Deborah R. Keen. Again, there were no qualifiers for a C.D.X. degree.

However, 1983 saw an upswing in Chows earning various titles. The following twenty-three completed the C.D. requirements: Boo-Boo Bear Bryant, Christine Ratekin and Gregory J. Volz; Chappell's Red Princess, James Frank Chappell; Ch. Charkay's Chivas Regal O'Jen-Lu, Mary Nitka; Criskoken Red Ruskin, Margaret R. Crisson; Cub Ty Kwi Ki, Katherie M. Willard; Emperor Keiki Kos, Adela Hergenreter; Ch. Fan-Ci Ravishing Ruby, Mary Ann Whitney; Gandalf, Stacy L. Land; Gotschall's Ebony Angel, Patricia L. Ingerham; Hei-Te An-Hsi-Jih Damien, Valerie H. Hoff; Hsiuing Kou, Fanne Ellner; Humphrey's Ebony Prince, Jeraldine A. and Larry F. Humphrey; June's Daisy May, June Patterson; Lady Scarlet of Cresson, Walter A. Felker; Lady Shih Ji, Sheree C. Chan; Ch. Los Cerros Roddie's Liu Mang, Cody and Myrna Milligan; Miss Leah Lee Chow, Susan H. Poythress; Mr. McBarker of Lorraine, Kim and Buft Lindemoen; Redcloud Mulberry, Zola Coogan and Bob and Joan Costello; Shogun's Empress K'wan, Mary L. Alexander; Su-J's The Midnight Mace, Sharon F. Batte; The Dove's Magichow, Dovie Lynn Trotter and Wally Wonka Chubbs, Thomas E. Shea, Jr.

Five Chows went on to earn a C.D.X.: Carolyn's Cinnamon Bear, Carolyn Scott; Jim Dandy's Teddy Bear, James W. Ingerham; Ng Ka Py, Catherine and Edmund Halley; Richard's Chelsea Belladona, Richard A. and Trina R. Marostica and Tien Ching Lady Nimshi, Sandra L. Allen.

Matthew's Momma Mei, CD, owned by Eamon M. Storrs added the Tracking Dog title to her name that year.

Twenty-six Chows earned their C.D. in 1984: Amber's Grizzly Bear, Fred and Leslie Petengill; Bexar de Palm, William M. George; Black China Bear II, Carl and Barbara A. Malone; Cathy's Li Sao Tai Sing, Mary Catherine Clapp; China's Pudgy Pooh Bear, John and Muriel J. Barrette; Dusty's Prince Coaldust, Virginia L. Criscitelli; Emperor Chowming West, Franklin G. West, Jr.; Jasmine Acklin, Kenn and Cindy Acklin; Julie-Lou's Ms. Pepper A-Chu, Julie L. Conine; Kucha Kai-Mo Shan, Karen E. Kibbell; Manchouli-Tu, Deborah R. and James L. Keen; Miss-Jean's Teak Would, Tracy Rhoads; Nanching Li Ij's Ching Ling, Irma Jean Murdock; Princess Ebony Chow Ming Su, Robert and Beverly Martell; Princess Jasming, Lori and Arlan Hartman; Red China III,

Fred and Martha Bunch; Rick-Su's Play It Agin Grump, James A. Steinmetz; Sasha, Terri L. Busher; Shel-Mar Shane of Char-Mar, Shelly L. Chrisman; Shel-Mar Teddy Bear, Richard J. and Lynn E. Croel; Sho-Tay's Hsiung Kow, Robert J. and Virginia Waszak; Stormi's Tumbleweed, Wanda Maywald; Sweet China Mist, Barbara and Carl Malone; Tai-Li Lohan of Taichung, Leonard A. Hanson and Douglas W. Johnston; The Wu Li Gypsy Rose, Meribeth Correll and Deborah R. Keene and Togotu, Vicki A. Storrs.

Qualifying for a C.D.X. degree were: Laurel Creeks Ginger Lady, for her owner, Carolyn J. Dyer and Suki-Tai, for Karen E. Kibbell.

In 1985, the Top Ten Obedience Chows were listed based on the total of their published scores. They were the following:

1 Miss Leah Lee Chow, C.D.X., *Poythress*
2 Shang Chiang Tang Mao Te, C.D., *Costanza*
3 Shelly's Din Bear, C.D., *Shelley*
4 Jim Dandy's Teddy Bear, U.D., *Ingerham*
5 Amber's Grizzly Bear, C.D.X., *Petengill*
6 Sweet China Mist, C.D.X., *Malone*
7 Ng Ka Py, U.D., *Halley*
8 Scotch Mist, C.D., *Skelton*
9 The Dove's Magichow, C.D., *Trotter*
10 Ingerham's Licorice Candy, C.D., *Ingerham*

During that year, there were Chows earning twenty-nine C.D., four C.D.X. and two U.D. degrees.

In 1986, the Top Ten Obedience Chow Chows were:

1 Jim Dandy's Teddy Bear, U.D., *Ingerham*
2 Shang Chiang Yang Mao Te, C.D.X., *Costanza*
3 Shoh-Dee II, C.D., *Halley*
4 Blanton's Grin and Bear It, C.D., *Blanton*
5 Hao Heathcliff Arthur, C.D., *Arthur*
6 Cojo Dragons I of The Tiger, C.D., *Ellner*
7 Sal Mae's Love Is The Answer, C.D., *Cuccia*
8 Little Rockum Sako of Xanadu, C.D., *DeBruyn*
9 Cassanova's Flashdance, C.D., *Blanton*
10 Sampson The Great VIII, C.D., *Carver*

There were twenty-six C.D. and three C.D.X. degrees earned by Chows that year.

Sophie goes directly to the articles for SCENT DISCRIMINATION, a Utility exercise.

Debbie gives Sophie the direction to the designated glove in DIRECTED RETRIEVE, a Utility exercise.

Sophie returns with the correct glove in DIRECTED RETRIEVE, a Utility exercise.

An Obedience Pictorial

The author is grateful to Deborah R. Keen and her Kansu obedience Chows for providing the photographs for this chapter. The Chows pictured demonstrating the various obedience exercises are: Chewli, Manchouli-Tu, C.D.; P'king, Wu Li's Peking Prince, C.D.; Sophie, The Wu Li Gypsy Rose, C.D.X.; Gypsy, Wu Li Gypsy Star of Kansu, D.C., and Shawn, Wu Li General Shan Kansu.

P'king recognizes and follows human scent for TRACKING. He's delighted when he finds the article at the end of the track.

At home, Ch. Teabear's Cheese Whizz shares the limelight with a few friends.

15

Chow Chows
in the Limelight

CHOWS HAVE WON the hearts of people from all walks of life. In the nineteenth century Queen Victoria of England had a pair which gave others incentive to consider this unique breed. A Chow resided in the White House during the 1923-1929 term of United States President Calvin Coolidge. This probably contributed to the popularity surge of Chows during the twenties and thirties. In the 1970's, Ohio Senator Wayne Hayes had his red Chow bitch successfully campaigned to group wins. President Reagan's Chief of Staff Howard Baker and former Pennsylvania Governor Milton Shapp are recognized as being Chow owners.

This author spoke with Todd Morgan who handles public relations for Graceland Division of Presley Enterprises. Mr. Morgan related how much Elvis Presley cared for all his pets, from monkeys to dogs. During the time Elvis was dating Linda Thompson, he owned a red Chow named Gitlow. The dog unfortunately suffered from a kidney ailment, so Elvis had his private pilot fly Gitlow from Memphis to Boston. The specialists in Boston were unable to save the Chow, and Elvis was left heartbroken.

In literature, you will find that Chow breeder-owner Konrad Lorenz included the breed in his *King Solomon's Ring*. *The Memoires of Chi-Chi* was a book published in the thirties about the Chow Chow Chi-Chi who lived the grand life with his owners, Mr. and Mrs. Berry Wall. For sixteen years, the travels of the Walls were related through Chi-Chi's point of view, although authored by Mrs. Wall. Caricatures of Mr. Wall and Chi-Chi showed both wearing high starched collars. When the aged Chow finally passed away, his widespread renown among the aristocracy and celebrities was cause for some French newspapers to carry an obituary for him.

In Dr. Imogene Earle's Maryland home hung a particularly serene photograph of the great artist Georgia O'Keeffe with her Pandee Chow beside her.

The founder of psychoanalysis, Dr. Sigmund Freud, must have found studying his Chows' personalities a challenge.

Television personalities who own Chows include Ron Glass of "Barney Miller" fame and Heather Lockleer of "Dynasty." Sally Struthers loves her Chow so much that she designed a poster of her Chow and daughter. It became part of the delightful Chow memorabilia that was sold at the 1987 National Specialty auction.

16

The Chow Chow Parent and Regional Clubs

THE CHOW CHOW CLUB, Inc. is also known as the CCC, Inc. or the Parent Club. It was organized in 1906 in Philadelphia, Pennsylvania, largely through the efforts of Dr. and Mrs. Henry Jarrett. Its purpose is to ". . . protect and advance the interests of the breed." By holding shows, offering awards and prizes, and developing and publishing a breed Standard, the CCC, Inc. has worked toward this end. It also publishes a quarterly magazine, formerly called "The Bulletin" and now named "Chow Life."

The early National Specialty Shows were usually held in conjunction with the Westminster weekend in New York City. In 1920, most of the 198 Chow entries braved a blizzard to attend the first one. The judge, Mr. Theodore Crane, selected Ning Poo for Best of Breed and gave Best Bitch to Ch. Windholme Wan Lung. Both winners were sired by a great dog of that era, Ch. Win Sum Min T'Sing.

Entries for the National continued to be high through the twenties and thirties when the Chow was peaking in popularity. The

CCC, Inc. attempted to hold two Specialties a year, the winter one in New York and a summer one on the grounds of Giralda Farms in New Jersey, the site of the Morris and Essex show. Then, as now, the annual meeting of the club was held in conjunction with the National.

Nowadays, the once-yearly National rotates throughout the four zones of the United States. The various regional clubs usually host it when it falls in their geographic zone.

During the week of the National Specialty, one can participate in Sweepstakes, Regular Classes, Obedience and Junior Showmanship judging. Clinics and seminars are offered for your edification in the breed. Socializing with Chowists from all over the world is one of the best learning experiences you will have.

The Parent Club's membership is mainly composed of United States residents. However, its roster also includes individuals from Canada, Japan, England and Norway.

The winners of the prestigious National Specialty Best of Breed in recent years include: 1975 in Reston, Va. under Mr. Louis Murr and 1976 in Denver, Colo. under Mr. C. L. Savage—Ch. Starcrest Lemon Drop Kid, breeders-owners Joel and June Marston; 1977 in Madison, Wis. under Mr. Percy Whitaker—Ch. Hanoi Tiko Topper, bred by Dulcie Smith and owned by J. C. F. Peddie and H. E. and J. I. Williams; 1978 in Reston, Va. under Mr. Joseph E. Gregory—Ch. Melody's Saint Noel, bred by Nola Davis and owned by Dan and Kim O'Donnell; 1979 in San Rafael, Calif. under Mr. Robert Waters—Ch. Cherie's Prince Kim Hi O'Jody, bred by Sherrie Harper and owned by L. Beryl Wical and Alfred L. Wical; 1980 in Phoenix, Ariz. under Mr. Frank Sabella—Can. and Am. Ch. Mi Tu's Han Su Shang, bred by Mrs. Pat Robb and owned by Herb and Joan Williams and Fred Peddie. This was a repeat of Shang's 1974 win under Mr. Isodore Schoenberg; 1981 in Edina, Minn. under Mr. Hiro Takagi—Ch. Teabear's Cheese Whizz bred and owned by L. J. Kip Kopatch; 1982 in North Grafton, Mass. under Mr. L. A. Entwistle—Ch. Wah-Hu Redcloud Sugar Daddy bred by Mary Ann Chambers and owned by Zola Coogan and Gloria Plunkett; 1983 in Beaverton, Oreg. under Mrs. Joan Egerton—Ch. Pinewood's Renaissance, bred and owned by George D. Boulton; 1984 in Northglen, Colo. under Mr. Clif Shryock—the bitch Ch. Cassanova's Isabelle, bed and owned by Julia B. Loratto; 1985 in Elgin, Ill. under Mr. Joseph E. Gregory—Ch. Claymont's New Edition of Noel, bred and owned by Rich, Kellie and JoAnn

Jaggie; 1986 in Atlanta, Ga. under Dr. Samuel Draper—Ch. Chinabear Gold Bullion, bred and owned by Gary and Carmen Blankenship and 1987 in Claremont, Calif. under Mr. Joel Marston —Ch. Jade West's Golden Boi, bred by R. F. Edmondson and owned by Alberta H. Edmondson. It is interesting to note that eleven out of the aforementioned fourteen wins were accomplished owner-handled.

Regional Clubs

Chowists in various parts of the country band together for the common goal of furthering the best interests of the Chow Chow. Some organizations have fallen by the wayside and others continue to stay together.

From a listing of then-active regional clubs in 1940, we see that, for instance, there no longer is a Montgomery County Chow Breeders Association, a Penn-Jersey Chow Chow Club, a Miami Valley Chow Chow Club or a Golden Bear Black Chow Chow Club. However, one of those on the list, Chow Fanciers' Association of Southern California, is the oldest, continuously-active regional Chow club in the country. It was organized in 1925 and was incorporated in 1927. Although it changed names along the way, from Chow Chow Club of the West to Greater CCC of California to Greater CCC of Southern California to its present CFA of Southern California, it is still with us. Another old regional club is on the East Coast, Southern CCC. It held its first Specialty show in 1926.

To find out which regional club are presently active in your area, first write to The American Kennel Club, 51 Madison Avenue, New York, NY 10010 and ask for the name and address of the Chow Chow Club, Inc.'s current corresponding secretary. He or she will then give you the secretaries' addresses of any of the following organizations you might want to consider joining. The list includes those clubs not yet recognized by the A.K.C. as well as those which are sanctioned or licensed to sponsor A.K.C. approval events.

Western Division—
North Texas Chow Chow Club*
CCC of Lubbock
CC Fanciers of South Texas
CCC of Greater Houston†
Copper State Chow Fanciers
Greater Phoenix CC Fanciers Association

253

Central Mexico CCC
Rocky Mountain CCC*
Pacific Northwest CCC*
CCC of Eastern Washington*
Mt. Hood CCC*
Redwood Coast CCC†
Golden State CCC*
CFA of Southern California*
Hawaiian CCC

Eastern Division—
New England CCC*
Southern CCC*
CCC of Greater New York*
Carolina CCC
CC Fanciers of Atlanta*
Derbytown CCC
Western Michigan CCC*
Mid States CCC*
Wisconsin CCC*
Greater Twin Cities CCC†

*denotes clubs that are licensed by the A.K.C. to hold Specialty shows.

†indicates clubs that are sanctioned by the A.K.C. to sponsor A.K.C. Match shows as of this writing.

Specialty Winners

Licensed regional clubs may hold a Specialty show either independently or in conjunction with an all-breed show. The winners of those shows were compiled in annual statistician's committee reports by Bill Atkinson and others who selflessly devote much of their time to Parent Club projects. Here, then, are the Best of Breed (BOB) and Best of Opposite Sex to Best of Breed (BOS) winners from the recent regional Specialties.

Golden State Chow Chow Club—4/28/79 under judge K. Stine with an entry of 54 Chows, BOB to Ch. Cherie's Prince Kim Hi O'Jody, BOS to Starcrest Noel Noel; 4/26/80 under Dr. W. S. Houpt with an entry of 41, BOB to Ch. Cherie's Prince Kim Hi O'Jody, BOS to Ch. Cherie's Jubilee of Rebelrun; 4/5/81 under C.

L. Savage with 39, BOB to Ch. Caron's Minstrel Man and BOS to Janvan's Silhouette of Cherie; 5/1/82 under C. Shyrock with 71, BOB to Ch. Teabear's Cheese Whizz and BOS to Ch. Cherie's Jubilee of Rebelrun; 4/28/84 under F. T. Sabella with 83, BOB to Ch. Sing Fu's The Canadian and BOS to Sunburst's Echo in Autumn; 4/30/83 under J. E. Gregory with 65, BOB to Ch. Cherie's Prince Kim Hi O'Jody and BOS to Ch. Sunburst's Ginger Snap; 4/27/85 under Mrs. H. A. Gray with 84, BOB to Ch. Sing Fu's The Canadian and BOS to Ch. Paramount's Shinook of JC.

Chow Fanciers' Association of Southern California—4/29/79 under C. E. Wheeler with 50, BOB to Ch. Cherie's Prince Kim Hi O'Jody and BOS to Ch. Ukong Fleur; 12/9/79 under Mrs. G. Kloeber with 17, BOB Ch. Caron's Minstrel Man and BOS to Darien's Arabella; 4/27/80 under R. L. Ayers with 47, BOB to Ch. Cherie's Prince Kim Hi O'Jody and BOS to Ch. Cherie's Jubilee of Rebelrun; 4/26/81 under H. E. Lee with 39, BOB to Ch. Don Lee Messiah and BOS to Janvan's Silhouette of Cherie; 5/2/82 under H. Van de Wouw with 67, BOB to Ch. Teabear's Cheese Whizz and BOS to Ch. Cherie's Jubilee of Rebelrun; 5/1/83 under T. Stevenson with 60, BOB to Ch. Cherie's Prince Kim Hi O'Jody and BOS to Ch. Cherie's Jubilee of Rebelrun; 4/27/84 under E. Egerton with 78, BOB to Ch. Sing Fu's The Canadian and BOS to Mi Pao's Angel and 4/26/85 under H. Tagaki with 87, BOB to Ch. Sing Fu's the Canadian and BOS to Ch. Paramount's Shinook of JC.

Pacific Northwest Chow Chow Club—8/5/79 under D. T. McMillan with 13, BOB to Ch. Pinewood's Renaissance and BOS to Ch. Starcrest's Stewart's Folly; 2/24/80 under A. E. Treen with 14, BOB to Ch. Silverstone's Cypress and BOS to Luck Be Gal Gamin; 3/1/81 under C. M. Mulock with 25, BOB to Ch. Pinewood's Renaissance and BOS to Ch. Luck Be Gal Gamin; 2/28/82 under C. E. Wheeler with 36, BOB to Ch. Silverstone's Cypress and BOS to Rik Sha El Cee; 2/27/83 under D. Welsh with 32, BOB to Ch. Silverstone's Dignity and BOS to Ch. Leatherwood Casey; 6/4/83 under Mrs. H. E. Lee with 122, BOB to Ch. Koby's Smudgy Son and BOS to Pinewood Bel Air; 6/10/84 under T. Stevenson with 31, BOB to Ch. Taichung Justin of Mike Mar and BOS to Koby's Pebbles; 8/18/85 under Mrs. M. A. Young with 32, BOB to Ch. Starcrest Thundergust and BOS to Jasman's Topaz from Taichung.

Chow Chow Club of Eastern Washington—5/25/79 under G. T. Fancy with 14, BOB to Ch. Pinewood's Renaissance and BOS to Hillcrest's Cho Cho San; 5/23/80 under R. Gilliland with 13, BOB to Ch. Pinewood's Renaissance and BOS to Pinewood's Kararah; 5/22/81 under M. T. L. Downing with 13, BOB to Ch. Pinewood's Renaissance and BOS to Taichung China Doll; 5/28/82 under H. H. Martin with 20, BOB to Ch. Pinewood's Renaissance and BOS to Choi Oi Miss Amyth; 5/27/83 under Dr. W. E. Field, Jr. with 17, BOB to Ch. Pinewood's Renaissance and BOS to Ch. Leatherwood's Casey; 11/27/83 under C. E. Wheeler with 19, BOB to Ch. Canton Quentin and BOS to Heart's Flower Blossom; 5/26/84 under Dr. W. S. Houpt, BOB to Ch. Pinewood's Big Red Machine and BOS to Robinhill Kriket of Tu Ka's; 11/25/84 under G. Weymouth with 9, BOB to Ch. Nelson's Mai Tai and BOS to Clarcastle Fu Whoa Jeh Kwoi and 5/24/85 under Mrs. V. Shryock with 32, BOB to Ch. Taichung Justin of Mike-Mar and BOS to Ch. Koby's Miss Tiffany of Tori.

North Texas Chow Chow Club—2/23/79 under J. L. Vaughters with 43, BOB to Ch. Tsang-Po's Bamboo Boy and BOS to Ch. Wildwood Cat Dancing; 9/22/79 under H. K. Bishop with 20, BOB to Lady M's Ezi Rider and BOS to Ch. Tiawin Sandcastle; 9/20/80 under N. Calicura with 16, BOB to Ch. Cedar Creek's D Drummer Boi and BOS to Brigadoon's Fancy Dreamer; 3/30/81 under R. Wills with 32, BOB to Ch. Cedar Creek's D Drummer Boi and BOS to Sundance Ping Li Shu; 3/26/82 under J. T. Bennett with 40, BOB to Ch. Pinewood I Am The Boss and BOS to Ch. Brigadoon's Fancy Dancer; 3/25/83 under Mrs. V. Shryock with 52, BOB to Ch. Rodon's Buddy X Lin Su and BOS to Ch. Chinabear Shadow Dancer; 3/23/84 under E. Egerton with 91, BOB to Sundance Wah Hu Royal Flush and BOS to Chinabear Champagne Bubbles and 3/22/85 under F. T. Sabella with 72, BOB to Ch. Sundance Wah-Hu Royal Flush and BOS to Ch. Dandylion Kuhlua 'N Cream.

Western Michigan Chow Chow Club—11/12/78 under Mrs. C. R. Whitlocke with 32, BOB to Ch. Fan C Crimson Tide and BOS to Ch. Charkay's Daisy May Palm; 11/11/79 under G. E. Carlton with 21, BOB to Ch. Charkay's Lord Calvert O'Palm and BOS to Bu Dynasty The Chelsea Bun; 11/9/80 under J. H. Cook with 20, BOB to Ch. Kwan Ching Rising Sun and BOS to Ch. Frelin's Hoi Fay; 11/8/81 under J. B. Patterson with 38, BOB to Ch. Plainacre's Yantzee of Kobys and BOS to Ch. Jenlu's Hello Dolly; 11/14/82 under Mrs. C. R. Whitlocke with 26, BOB to Ch. Plainacre's Yantzee of Kobys and BOS to Ch. Claymont's Litany; 5/28/83 under Mrs. T. Stevenson with 47, BOB to Ch. Charkay's Grand Marnier O'Palm and BOS to Bu Dynasty The African Queen; 5/26/84 under C. M. Mulock with 36, BOB to Charkay's Grand Marnier O'Palm and BOS to Ch. Chi Debut's Metz's Sue Ellen and 5/25/85 under Mrs. R. H. Ward with 36, BOB to Ch. Mang Ti's Magnum Royale and BOS to Ch. Chi Debut's Metz's Sue Ellen.

Mid-States Chow Chow Club—3/30/79 under D. Duggins with 21, BOB to Ch. Melody's Rustic Rhythm and BOS to Lin Su's Rosie Posie of Rodon; 3/28/80 uner A. E. Treen with 18, BOB to Charkay's Ruby Chablis O'Palm and BOS to Ch. Kwan Ching Rising Sun; 3/27/81 under Dr. S. Draper with 33, BOB to Ch. Jen Sen's China Bear of Palm and BOS to CC's Hon E Bear of Carols; 4/2/82 under Dr. A. H. Reinitz with 23, BOB to Ch. Foon Ying Famous Amos and BOS to Twenty Four Karat of Chia Hsi; 4/1/83 under K. O. Peterson with 47, BOB to Ch. Claymont's New Edition of Noel and BOS to Ch. Claymont's Litany; 3/30/84 under F. P. A. Odenkirchen with 40, BOB to Tamarin Red Puzzle Foon Ying and BOS to Ch. Sher Ron's Sara Lea and 6/7/85 under E. E. Bivin with 90, BOB to Ch. Moonwynd Abracadabra and BOS to Chia Hsi Go For The Gold.

Wisconsin Chow Chow Club—7/1/79 under Miss M. V. Beam with 21, BOB to Ch. Sharbo Sunnybrook Beau Geste and BOS to Ch. Charkay's Daisy May Palm; 6/29/80 under E. R. Klinckhardt with 14, BOB to Ch. Rodon's Mr. Chips and BOS to Ch. Rodon's Pooh Bear; 6/28/81 under Mrs. V. Shryock with 14, BOB to Ch. Buddy Budweiser of Sunny Oak and BOS to Heritage Georgie Girl; 5/9/82 under Mrs. J. Fancy with 13, BOB to Ch. Charkay's Grand Marnier O'Palm and BOS to Sharbo Belcase; 5/8/83 under Mrs. N. P. Riley with 15, BOB to Ch. Charkay's Grand Marnier O'Palm and BOS to Charkay's Bianco; 5/6/84 under Dr. A. H. Reinitz with 14, BOB to Ch. Charkay's Grand Marnier O'Palm and BOS to Chia Hsi Country Gold and 5/5/85 under Mrs. L. B. Weisman with 16, BOB to Palm's Boogie Woogie Boy and BOS to Chia Hsi Go For The Gold.

Southern Chow Chow Club—3/11/79 under Dr. S. Remmele with 32, BOB to Ch. Teabear's Cheese Whizz and BOS to Moonwynd Heaven Sent; 3/9/80 under H. E. Lee with 58, BOB to

Ch. Jazmyn Solo Performance and BOS to Ch. Imperial Allegro; 4/18/81 under J. E. Frank with 43, BOB to Ch. Teabear's Cheese Whizz and BOS to Ch. Pandee's Artemis; 4/24/82 under H. Van de Wouw with 51, BOB to Ch. Teabear's Cheese Whizz and BOS to Ch. Laral's Tatiana; 4/23/83 under Miss V. E. Sivori with 43, BOB to Ch. Koby Cassanova of Sweetkins and BOS to Ch. Cassanova's Isabelle; 4/21/84 under J. G. Reynolds with 54, BOB to Ch. Wah Hu Redcloud Sugar Daddy and BOS to Ch. Kido's Buttercup and 4/20/85 under E. Egerton with 59, BOB to Ch. Moonwynd After Midnight and BOS to Ch. Pei-Gan Maxim of Redcloud.

Chow Chow Club of Greater New York—first annual show 5/19/85 under Mrs. P. M. Marcmann with 36, BOB to Domino Flying Tiger and BOS to Liontamer Redcloud Marilyn.

New England Chow Chow Club, Inc.—6/2/79 under C. Shryock with 51, BOB to Ch. Teabear's Cheese Whizz and BOS to Ch. Imperial Allegro; 5/31/80 under J. E. Gregory with 43, BOB to Ch. Teabear's Cheese Whizz and BOS to Ch. Starcrest Baltimore Oriole; 5/30/81 under Mrs. C. Whitlocke with 33, BOB to Ch. Dusten's Anticipation and BOS to Applewood's Umee; 6/5/82 under F. P. A. Odenkirchen with 76, BOB to Ch. Teabear's Cheese Whizz and BOS to Ch. Cherie's Jubilee of Rebelrun; 11/27/83 under Dr. S. Draper with 33, BOB to Ch. Redcloud Sylvan Sky Walker and BOS to Ch. Mityme's Autumn Sunset; 6/2/84 under J. G. Reynolds with 27, BOB to Ch. Wah Hu Redcloud Sugar Daddy and BOS to Ch. Wah Hu Angel of The Morning and 6/1/85 under Mrs. S. B. Tietjen with 26, BOB to Ch. Redcloud Sylvan Sky Walker and BOS to Ch. Milu's Continental Grace.

17

The Chow Chow in Art

T HE ARTISTIC RENDERING of Chows is always a challenge to artists in any medium. One must find form under the fluff, so to speak. So, whether it is a bronze, an oil, a lithograph, a stamp, a wood carving or a ceramic modeled on a Chow, it's worth collecting.

With the two fad periods the breed has experienced, there has been a proportionately high volume of work produced. For some reason, however, these pieces are not readily apparent in antique shops, flea markets and auction houses yet. It is probable that the owners of Chows and the keepsakes thereof are still with us and holding on to their collections. So, amidst the present flood of Chow items on the market today, your purchase now may be an heirloom tomorrow.

The following pieces of Chow art and crafts are mostly from collections of Paul and Minnie Odenkirchen and that of this author.

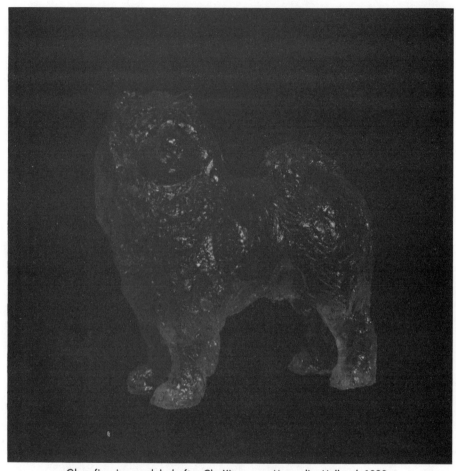

Glass figurine modeled after Ch. Xingu van Mongolie, Holland, 1980.
Odenkirchen

Royal Copenhagen porcelain figurine #4762, Denmark, 1979, modeled after Danish Ch. Zoto's
Emperor of Liang-Ming-Keou, Holland.   *Odenkirchen*

A bas-relief wall hanging sculpted from the hair of a blue Chow Chow. *Koby*

1980 Australian wood carving #1 in a series of four, commissioned by Shelly and Scott Steckly and modeled after Can. Am. Ch. Mi-Pao's Timang. *Odenkirchen*

"Devotion," clay model by Jim Sawyer, USA, 1982.   *Odenkirchen*

Three ceramics: #38 by Ron Hevener, USA, 1982; Jie, Sweden, 1972 and #29 by Ron Hevener, USA, 1983.

Odenkirchen

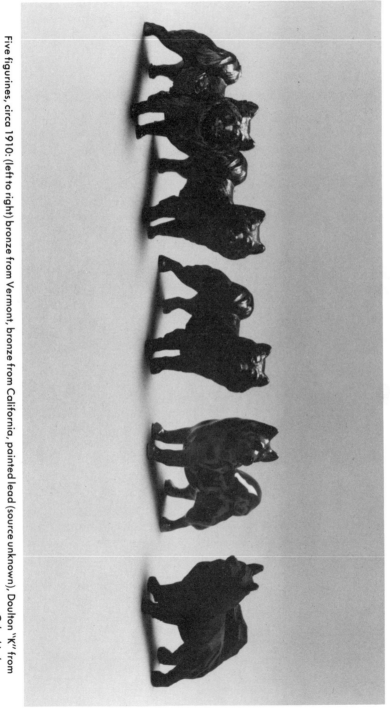

Five figurines, circa 1910: (left to right) bronze from Vermont, bronze from California, painted lead (source unknown), Doulton "K" from England and wood from Italy.

West Coast ceramic, circa 1940, donated by Dr. Jo Anne O'Brien and D.K. Dennis, ceramic, USA, 1979.   *Odenkirchen*

A handpainted, porcelain tea set, Sonya Rood, 1981.   *Kip*

Two Jan Allan figurines, circa 1940.

Part of the private collection in the home of Paul and Minnie Odenkirchen.

Odenkirchen

More collectibles belonging to Paul and Minnie Odenkirchen.   *Odenkirchen*

Black, red and blue ceramic figurines by Stan Smedley, Junggwaw, England, 1980.

Odenkirchen

Alabaster French figurine donated by Mrs. Mimpen, Holland.
Odenkirchen

A variety of pins and pendants owned by Mi-Pao Kennels, Canada. *Odenkirchen*

Copper by Hiroshi Takagi, Japan, 1980.   *Odenkirchen*

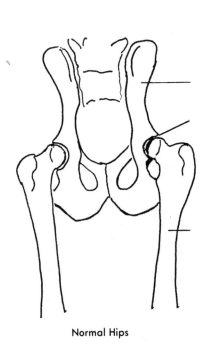

Normal Hips

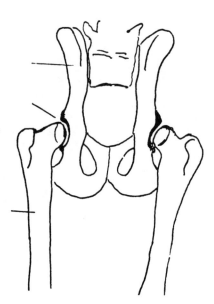

Moderate Dysplasia

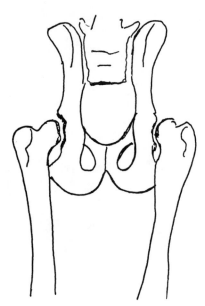

Severe Dysplasia

18

Hip Dysplasia Control
for Chows

AS STATED IN AN earlier chapter, all parts of the
Chow must be taken into consideration when evaluating the whole
dog. There are certain attributes and faults that can be seen with the
naked eye or felt by hand. Other things can be determined only by
the use of instruments or radiography. From Adie Toudt, the
Orthopedic Foundation for Animals representative for the Parent
Club comes the following:

"The term Hip Dysplasia refers to the improper development of
the hip joint. It is an inherited trait controlled by the genetic makeup
of the individual dog, with degrees of severity that manifest
themselves in different ways. Some affected dogs may show little or
no sign of discomfort while others with the same degree of severity
may be clinically disabled. It should not be assumed that this is a
totally progressive disease that shows up in an aging animal because
it is known that crippling hip irregularities were noted in puppies as
early as three months of age."

Hip problems in the dog were first recognized in 1935 and
research began soon after. The Orthopedic Foundation for Animals

(OFA) came into being in the 1960's. It was this organization that made it possible to obtain a more uniform interpretation of the radiographic films. Control programs were started in most of the breed clubs, including regional and the national Chow clubs. Affected Chows were detected through radiography and "the importance of knowing" took on a new meaning.

The first Chow Chow was entered into the OFA Registry in 1968 and only a few were added each year until the importance was confirmed. Currently there are nearly 1,200 Chow Chows registered by the OFA. Impressive progeny lists attest to the fact that like-begets-like.

Recently, the Chow Chow Club, Inc. added "OFA Certification" to the list of qualifications for the eligibility for Supreme Chow and other top annual awards.

Until scientists and researchers discover other causes, and alternative methods of detection, breeders should be aware of the positive approach to the elimination of the disease by controlling it through radiographic findings and OFA verification.

OFA Certified Chow Chows

The following list of almost 1,200 Chows whose hips were graded to be good enough to be assigned an OFA number was painstakingly typed by Mrs. Toudt.

OFA # CC	OFA # CC
1 — Ch. Elster's Gee Nee Of Chia Hsi	19 — Wah-Hu's Hi-Hi
2 — Ch. Wah Hu's Image of Buddha	20 — Ch. Wah-Hu's Brass Buddha
3 — Ch. Ky-Lin's Red Buddha	21 — Ch. Pandee's Double Jubilee
4 — Ch. Playin' Jane of Chia Hsi	22 — Ch. Don-Lee's Prophet
5 — The Red Baron Of Chia Hsi	23 — Ch. Don-Lee's Q-Tee De Krikett
6 — Ch. Palm's Lucy of Chia Hsi	24 — Red Fugui
7 — De Selwonk's Gray Chan of China	25 — Ch. Starcrest Miss Chrissy
8 — Ch. Kan King's Charlie Wong	26 — Leander Mairim Mitzi Tu
9 — Miss May of Chia Hsi	27 — Ch. Leander His Nibs
10 — Palm's Sue Ling	28 — Palm's Ebony Queen
11 — Sandune's Rlow Kai	29 — King's Lian Ningtu
12 — Tahg Along of Chia Hsi	30 — Ch. Jade's Miss Hu-Cat Ballou
13 — Palm's Miss Chubby	31 — Ch. Pandee's U-Doll
14 — G. R. Owl's Ging Chat of Landon	32 — Yu Hu AR D Devil Packer
15 — Palm's Cissy of Hillside	33 — Palm's Chang of Wu T'sai
16 — Palm's Love of Wu T'Sai	34 — Ro-Jo's Ming Toy
17 — Ch. Pandee's Tillitha	35 — Kan King's Jingles
18 — Ch. Gotschall's Chang Kou Chian	36 — Ch. Charmar Red Dragon Tu

37 — Sharbo Pocho
38 — Ky-Lin's Black Star
39 — Ch. Royal Rin's Licorice Candy
40 — Sharbo Tai Sha
41 — Ch. Starcrest Bewitched of Ho-San
42 — Ch. Don-Lee's Jubilee
43 — Palm's Peppermint Patty
44 — Ky-Lin's Na-Ka-De
45 — Ch. Ro-Jo's Ric-A-Tic
46 — Ch. Liontamer Mardi Gras
47 — Ch. Starcrest By Jupiter O'Sharbo
48 —
49 — Pandee's Cin Nee Witch
50 — Pandee's Lunette
51 — Pandee's Klarion
52 — Pandee's Katanga
53 — Ch. Don-Lee's Jewel of Ho-San
54 — Elster's Fortune Koo Kee
55 — Livin'Doll of Poppyland
56 — Lu Chow's Patsy Hsing
57 — Starcrest Q.P. Doll of Don-Lee
58 — Pandee's Xenia
59 — Don-Lee's Kahlua of Eastward
60 — Ch. Don-Lee's Miscue of Gino's
61 — Don-Lee's Judi
62 — Ch. Starcrest Eastward Roman
63 — Titus Pandee Van Mongolie
64 — Pandee's Miss Smarty
65 — Pandee's Mischief
66 — Pandee's Silhouette
67 — Kan King's Black Knight
68 — Charmar's Ding Ling
69 — Ch. Gino's Chang Hai
70 — Pandee's Sargossa
71 — Pandee's Sabrina
72 — Pandee's Sailor Girl
73 — Pandee's Zephyr of Keibler
74 — Ch. Pandee's Meeko
75 — Pandee's Genghis
76 — Pandee's Khublar
77 — Von Packette's Pooh of Keibler
78 — Mar-Su's-Mao-Chin
79 — Eastward Liontamer Lucy
80 — Ch. Kan King's Charm
81 —
82 — Ch. Starcrest Matinee Idol
83 — Mi-Star-Ling-Tu
84 — Ch. Shamrock's Golden Nuggett

85 — Starcrest Jupiter of Pandee
86 — Ch. Starcrest Mr. Christopher
87 — Pandee's Yma
88 — Pandee's Shen Valee
89 — Tsang-Po's Linn Fu Chang
90 — Ch. Sharbo's Satanya
91 — Sharbo Black Magic
92 — Candy Winnie Poo of Sharbo
93 — Ch. Starcrest Dandy Lion
94 — Ch. Starcrest Fros-Tee
95 — Ch. Su-To's Charlie Chan
96 — Eastward Blockade
97 — Eastward Mona of Pandee
98 — Chubby Von Thiele
99 — Ch. Tsang-Po's So-Pai-Chee
100 — Ch. Tsang-Po's Linn Fu Yi
101 — Carchow's Tu Shuz Tish
102 — Pandee's Blu Witching
103 — Ch. Starcrest Bam Bam
104 — Ro-Jo
105 — Ch. Kwan Rei's Shorty Short Stuff
106 — Ch. Sharbo's Mutluk
107 — Ch. Sarbo Image of The Dragon
108 — Pandee's Sunny Lass
109 — Starcrest Cameo
110 — Ch. Ro-Lo Anastasia of Starcrest
111 — Ch. Ro-Jo's Jeri Lu-Ling
112 — Kanchow Kailan
113 — Palm's Lum of Hillside
114 — Starcrest Lemon Twist
115 — Carla Charlene
116 — Ch. Rivendell's Nicholas
117 — Ch. Shamrock's Klan-Cee
118 — Mitsu Bee Lairson
119 — Kan King's Pudgy
120 — Sharbo's Merry Holiday
121 — Tsang-Po's Chung Su Kim
122 — Wi-Ro's Lisa of Wah-Hu
123 — Ch. Wah-Hu's Chutzpah
124 — Wah-Hu's Brass Buttons
125 — Wah-Hu's Chinese Cheesecake
126 — Charisma of Chia Hsi
127 — Dark Cloud Chia Hsi Martonge
128 —
129 — Lli Haven's Penny Lee
130 — Black Magic of Chia Hsi
131 — Tina's Hol-Lee of Chia Hsi
132 — Don-Lee's Tiffany of Caron

133 — Mai Lai of Mingodell
134 — Ch. Ah-Sid Liontamer Jamboree
135 — Plainacre's Silhouette
136 — Ch. Plainacre's Holy Smoke
137 — Ch. Tamarin Ch'ing Lung
138 — Chu Ling of Selwan-Lu
139 — Ch. Lawson's Hey Lien Dande Boi
140 — Ky-Lin's Simba
141 — Ch. Dre-Don's Miss Caledonia
142 — Ch. Dre-Don's Dinah Dee
143 — Ch. Dre-Don's Gidget of Wong-Sui
144 — Ch. Tsang-Po's Travelin Man Carchow
145 — Soo-Zoo-Ky
146 — Wun Dae's Kashana Kava
147 — Ch. Snowden's Arkansas Special
148 — Ch. Liontamer Bruiser
149 — Lli Haven Black Jack
150 — Ch. Don-Lee's Peppermint Patty
151 — Ch. Don-Lee's Umbo of Chia Hsi
152 — Millers Black Gin Tina
153 — Ch. Starcrest Top Cat
154 — Ch. Jo-Lew's Mung Wutso of Car-Lin
155 — Ch. Tush-Pish of Dun-E-Dene
156 — Cherie's Twilight Trojan
157 — Starcrest Liontamer Memoire
158 — Ch. Wah-Hu's Fo Kuang
159 — Five Ash Top Flight
160 — Ding-Ah-Ling of Chia Hsi
161 — Ch. Starcrest Lemon Drop Kid
162 — Ch. Starcrest Andy of Lu-Hi
163 — Ch. Don-Lee's Uneek Luvin' Doll
164 — Ch. Swain's Amethyst of Chia Hsi
165 — Princess Ginger Flower
166 — Mae Lin Sal
167 — Ch. Hung Jai Lin Fa, U.D.
168 — Hue Weh of Chia Hsi
169 — Cabill's Dandi Girl
170 — Miller's Smokey Baron
171 — Ch. Tinum Yulu Tulu of Chia Hsi
172 — Ch. Palm's Raygo of B and B
173 — Ch. Stewart's Primo
174 — Ming-Too
175 — Justamere's Rouge Promise
176 — Inkey Poo
177 — Van Zotte of Chia Hsi
178 — Ch. Lile Lotus Blossom of Lil-Herm
179 — Lu-Kee Tian of Prophet
180 — Keegan's Mala Chang

181 — L'Li Haven's Lil Bit O'Starcrest
182 — Ch. Chia Hsi Black Beary Supreme
183 — Don-Lee's Luxury Lace
184 — Sylvan Queen of Chia Hsi
185 — Starcrest Tea Rose
186 — Ch. Jemaco Ho-Tei of Nether-Lair
187 — Ch. Ro-Jo's Brandy
188 — Cherie's Sunkissed Mist
189 — Miller's Scott Blue Chang
190 — Pandee's Amanda of Tamarin
191 — Tamarin Black Baron
192 — Lli Haven's Ming of Starcrest
193 — Ch. Don-Lee's Ching Ling
194 — Ukwong Playboy
195 — Ch. Cabaret Candy Man
196 — Ch. Cabaret Blackjack
197 — Ch. Gottschall's Miss Personality
198 — Ch. Frelin's Fan-C Wun Gottschall
199 — Ch. Audrich Ebony of Cabaret
200 — Starcrest Bruin of Brylea
201 — Ch. Starcrest Ego
202 — Ch. Fa-Ci Aspen
203 — Ch. Starcrest Titan O'Wilderland
204 — Ch. Nan-Li's Red Fred
205 — Ch. Pandee's Jayetta
206 — Ch. Cherie's Firewind Fiesta
207 — Ch. Cabaret Ruby J
208 — Palm's Image of Ebony
209 — Palm's King Sampson
210 — Wah-Hu's Ho-Toi of Lomac
211 — Ch. Sharbo The Catalyst
212 — Ch. Sharbo The Dictator
213 — Pandee's Jubilation
214 — Ch. Sharbo Talisman
215 — Ch. Sum Buddha's Edlen Shu Gar
216 — Ch. Melody's Saint Noel
217 — Waymar's Most Precocious
218 — Pa-Kum's Leuchow
219 — Ch. Sumthin Difrent of Braeside
220 — Wah-Hu's Shine On
221 — Five Ash Honey Bear
222 — Five Ash Hi Smoke
223 — Ch. Ro-Jo Lamont Cranston
224 — Ch. Rob Loi Cameo By Prophet
225 — Starcrest Bravo Crystalton
226 — Ch. Imperial Caprice of Chia Hsi
227 — Ch. Cabaret Joker
228 — Ch. Tsang-Po's Storm Trooper

229 — Kanzaki's Mari Oso
230 — Ch. Liontamer Sunrise of Palm
231 — Liontamer Sunbonnet of Palm
232 — Ch. Tsang-Po's Daquiri
233 — The Duke of Chia Hsi
234 — Ch. Charkay's Contessa of Chia Hsi
235 — Swain's Atam of Chia Hsi
236 — Applewood's Ziphia, C.D.
237 — Sharbo Miss Priss of Justamere
238 — Ch. Sharbo The Premier
239 — Sharbot The Harlot
240 — Sharbo The Sorceress
241 — Ch. Sharbo Sunnybrook Shady Lady
242 — Gypsy Wo Home
243 — Boblu Moody Blues
244 — Neb Sar Ka Ling
245 — Ch. Lakeview's Mr. T
246 — Winbar's Moon Shadow
247 — Ch. Frelin Priscilla
248 — Ch. Frelin's Ruby A of Shang Ti
249 — Ch. Lil Haven Hell N Redi of Sal Mae
250 — Ch. Tsang Po's Motsu Inu
251 — Starcrest Tigress
252 — Cabaret Royal Flush
253 — Cabaret Dealers Choice
254 — Ch. Cherie's Chablis O'Prophet
255 — Ch. Hyjinx Ms Tikopin
256 — Ch. Palm's Little Faith
257 — Ch. Bo Chang
258 — Tao Ming's Apache Windsong
259 — Ch. Gottschall's Lucky of Frelin
260 — Sal Mae's Hidee of Lli Haven
261 — Ch. Wah-Hu's Sweet Tzu
262 — Ch. Cherie's Prince Kim Hi O'Jody
263 — Fizzwick Earl of Sunburst
264 — Shamrock Luv Is Blu Jemaco
265 — Ch. Chinabear Merrigold
266 — Ch. Dre-Don's Diamond Drop
267 — Ch. Gotschall's Red Topper
268 — Gotschall's Justice of Frelin
269 — Ch. Imperial Allegro
270 — Pandee's Yuan Yin Ming
271 — Brandy The 11th
272 — Ch. Cape Fear Luv-Chow's Ai Jen, C.D.
273 — Swain's Margo Margot
274 — Ch. Cabaret Hustler
275 — Chinabear Lotus Blossom
276 — Ro Jean's Chisum of Debchow

277 — Starcrest Kid Napper
278 — Jemaco Mr. Blu-Ti Full
279 — Hanchow's Wu-Tip
280 — Starcrest Luv Bug
281 — Miller's Blue Smoke
282 — Justamere's Frank Lee Scarlett
283 — Ch. Liontamer Alexander De Palm
284 — Brenda Star of Chia Hsi
285 — Rhoda of Chia Hsi
286 — Cassanova's Samson
287 — Taibel Blazing Glory
288 — Holland's Midnight Magician
289 — Shelly's Ms D-Lyla Beowulf
290 — Ch. Diamond Jim Blake
291 — Ch. Woolie Wonka of Wah-Hu
292 — Mee Too of Wah-Hu
293 — Boblu Chocolate Mousse
294 — Ch. Boblu Burgandy Bear Jung
295 — Ch. Kwi Chaing Tei-Meu Jin
296 — Wah-Hu's Midnight Star
297 — Chaling of Kaishan
298 — Weise Happi of Chia Hsi
299 — Boblu Arka Special Edition
300 — One For The Road of Chia Hsi
301 — Chia Hsi Wynken Sweetheart
302 — Kitty Van Grady of Chia Hsi
303 — Hanchow's Cleopatra
304 — Ch. Charkay's Daisy May Palm
305 — Poo Duke's Mao Ro Sz
306 — Ch. Redcloud's Fortunate Cookie
307 — Ch. Mang Ao Ring Master of Palm
308 — Mang Ao Ringside Gasip of Palm
309 — Wah-Hu Lorien Tsu Shih
310 — Ch. Little Miss Mufett Shi-Lai
311 — Ch. Don-Lee Chowtime
312 — Hanchow's Bagatelle
313 — Ch. Hanchow's Pee Chin
314 — Cabaret Maggie Mae
315 — Pandee's Piper Dream
316 — Shei-Lai's Blueberry Muffin
317 — Ch. Woolee Wonka's Rock Candy
318 — Liontamer Fluffy of Ho-San
319 — Gammon's Kate of Chia Hsi
320 — Ba Ba Blacksheep
321 — Ch. Gatewood Black Magic
322 — Ch. Starcrest Miss Ping Pong
323 — Jemaco Sandsation O'Pinewood
324 — Ah-Sid Ki Chow

325 — Ch. Blake No Regrets
326 — Rahiza Her Royal Lioness
327 — Lli Haven Mr. Volvo of Sal Mae
328 — Ch. Sharbo Sunnybrook Beau Geste
329 — Midnight Lady Onassis
330 — Hyjinx Bittersweet
331 — Miller's Trooper of Chia Hsi
332 — Waulee Lo Hu Po of Diana Lee
333 — Five Ash Victoria II
334 — Rodon's Fleetwood Mac
335 — Applewood's Velvet of Chia Hsi
336 — Wah-Hu's Ju Lee
337 — Palm's Liontamer Chrissy
338 — Palm's Liontamer Janet
339 — Ch. Dychow Chug-A-Mug
340 — Bu Dynasty The Star of The East
341 — Jewell's Blu Contessi
342 — Jewell's Supermanchu
343 — Palm's Liontamer Gem of B and B
344 — Palm's Black Pepper of B and B
345 — Sta-Cee's Shei-Lai Lorelei
346 — Ch. Frelin's Madame Wu
347 — Roses Are Red of Chia Hsi
348 — Violets Are Blue of Chia Hsi
349 — Ch. Carchow Boss Man
350 — Yu R Tu of Chia Hsi
351 — Ch. Miller's Odin of Hyjinx
352 — Miller's Chiffon of Starcrest
353 — Cherie's Black Gammon
354 — Applewood's Waldo
355 — Applewood's Wren
356 — Kamara Gypsy Boots
357 — Ch. Sta-Cee's Dandy Pandee
358 — Ch. Blu-Gras-Moses-O'-Cedar-Creek
359 — Ebony's Proud Lady, C.D.
360 — Cabaret Hel-Lo Devil Doll
361 — Ch. Valric Place-Ur Bets Of Don-Lee
362 — Ch. Valric Prophet Sharon
363 — Sunshine Miss Sunshine
364 — Gammon's Zipporah of Chia Hsi
365 — San-Ku's Miss Me
366 — Ch. Checkmate's Magic Mandy
367 — Ch. Scotchow Sheer Delight
368 — Ch. Starcrest Top Hat
369 — Ch. Justamere's Blu-Min-Rose
370 — Sparkles Plenty of Chia Hsi
371 — Ch. Griffchow's Sunny Sunshine
372 — Ch. Rodon's Pooh Bear

373 — Ch. Palm's Coquette
374 — Ch. Palm's Personality Kid
375 — Ch. Little Sunshine Ms Sunshine Shei-Lai
376 — Cedar Creek's Lu Shan
377 — All That Glitters of Chia Hsi
378 — Ch. Jemaco Jubilee Joanne
379 — Ch. Cherie's Blue Blazes of Janvan
380 — Ch. Tsang-Po's Bamboo Boy
381 — Shei-Lai Inky Dink
382 — Imperial Gypsy Moon Osa
383 — El Perro Ozo's
384 — Kamara Midnight Express
385 — Gotschall's Admiral Luvchow
386 — Sangate's Amal Kisky
387 — Genie of The Red Coats
388 — Ch. Cherie's Jubilee of Rebelrun
389 — Ch. Jonel's Track Mac Tavish
390 — Valric's Zorina of Tar Ram
391 — Woodrock Jessica of Tar Ram
392 — Ch. Pinewood's I Am The Boss
393 — Mi Pao's Echo Wood Elsa
394 — Bu Dynasty Courtessan
395 — Ch. Cherie's Hannibal of St. Noel
396 — Shane Lang Wong
397 — Woodrock Empress of Prophet
398 — Woodrock Prophet Elijah
399 — Ch. Woodrock Joy
400 — Ch. Woodrock Pride
401 — Woodrock Phil of Prophet
402 — Chow Chow Brown Sugar Shei-Lai
403 — Canton's San Suki
404 — Spindrift Cuddle Me Too
405 — Ch. Pinewood's Renaissance
406 — Liontmer Showtime Sadie
407 — Mi Tonka's Gin Sling of Wu Li
408 — Charkay's Pinot Noir
409 — Woodrock Pantages
410 — Taro's Osa Negro
411 — Ch. Jen-Sen's China Bear of Palm
412 — Mang Ao Queen of Spades
413 — Jen-Sen's Fox Fire of Palm
414 — Ch. Dentong Copper Boi
415 — (Duplicate — Reissued as #483)
416 — Ch. Dychow Ebony Soupie Tu
417 — Ch. Cedar Creek's Ms Chiona
418 — Hanchow Desiree
419 — Ch. Chinabear Chaz
420 — Kamara Prophecy

421 — Emperor Taurus Tong Sing
422 — Avatar Ling Bear
423 — Imperial Pandee of Liontamer
424 — Jenna's Bearfoot Contessa
425 — Ch. Palm's Block Buster
426 — Ch. Rebelrun's Jessica
427 — Kamara Joy To The World
428 — Kamara Yogi Bear
429 — Kamara Kudzu
430 — Ch. Mang Ao Babee Doll O'Palm
431 — Ch. Plainacre's Cameo Cover Girl
432 — Gammon's Kfir Marf of Chia Hsi
433 — Ch. Kamodan's Black Bart O'Palm
434 — Seawind's Blue-Belle
435 — Cedar Creek's Summer
436 — Kamps Shanti of Chia Hsi
437 — Ch. Checkmates Vision O'Grandeur
438 — Go-Sing The Entertainer
439 — Ginger Marie
440 — Mi-Pao's Roman Centurion
441 — Mi-Pao's Nocturna
442 — Rik-Sha Din-O-Mite
443 — Mi-Pao's Antiga
444 — Zebdee Majic Gem
445 — Pandee's Blooey O'Palm
446 — Go-Sing Portrait of Jenny
447 — Ch. Cedar Creek's Midnite Special
448 — Princess Mi Lan
449 — Ch. Jonel's Charlie
450 — Carolanda Tedi-Bear
451 — Cedar Creek's Maranatha
452 — Chinabear Arieanne
453 — Ch. Checkmate's Golden Girl
454 — Ch. Laral's Excalibur By Weiss
455 — Ch. Plainacre's Rock Me Tu
456 — Redcloud Temujin
457 — Jewell's Daisy A Day of Su-K
458 — Mi-Pao's Inhah
459 — Eastward Traveler
460 — Ch. Brigadoon's Fancy Dancer
461 — Starcrest Tiki Blue Pooh
462 — Sal Mae's Chin Chin Ping Soo
463 — Koby's Madame Ming
464 — Ch. Cedar Creek's Love-N-Licks
465 — Ch. Sparkling Ingot of Chia Hsi
466 — Ch. Barkwood Ounce of Gold
467 — Eastward Gypsy
468 — Ch. Cedar Creek's Ko-Di-Ak

469 — Jolin Ming Soo Chan
470 — Mi-Tu's Ebony Tide
471 — Ch. Charkay's Grand Marnier O'Palm
472 — Mi-Pao's Taichung Magic
473 — Tasha of Don-Rae
474 — Woodrock Aloha
475 — Luvchow Liontamer Bloosom
476 — Teabear Pattycake Pattycake
477 — Ch. Sal Mae's Comin Up Roses
478 — Profit's Blessing
479 — Imperial Ode
480 — Ghengis Khan 12
481 — Elkomac Merry Enchantress
482 — Dychow Vashti Bera Kaii Tu
483 — Dychow Kapt'n Krunch Tu
484 — Mugs-A-Plenty of Chia Hsi
485 — Eastward Bandit
486 — Ch. Bondsai's Fantasia De Saint
487 — Ch. Starcrest Rainbow
488 — Shin-Yi of Palm
489 — Ch. Palm's One In A Million
490 — Kamara King Creole
491 — Jung's Strawberry Shortcake
492 — Sugar Mao of Texas
493 — Ch. Pinewood Pharoah of Venus
494 — Leatherwood Kadiz
495 — Satan's Dandy Bear
496 — Ch. Cedar Creek's Mystic Jade
497 — Jen-Lu's Sunny Taipan
498 — Kwan Eln's Fortune
499 — Charkay's Chateau La Salle
500 — Ch. Claymont's Christmas In July
501 — Carrie Moon Beamer
502 — Ch. Bondsai's Mizzou De Saint
503 — Ch. Plainacre's Wen Su of Kobys
504 — Mary Ann's Ching-Ho-Che-Miam
505 — Mister Bear's Meng Toi
506 — Bonnie Peach of Carolanda
507 — Chia Hsi Black Mistique
508 — Tao-Ming's TNT
509 — Ch. Cabaret Cracker Jack
510 — Ch. Cedar Creek's Ginger Cookie
511 — Brindy Boo
512 — Chow-Li Chan of Chia Hsi
513 — Ch. Claymont's New Edition of Noel
514 — Ch. Plainacre's Mischief Maker
515 — Ch. Marian's Imperial Pandy Bear
516 — Palm's Midnight Magic

517 — Palm's Junior Bear
518 — Ch. Checkmate's Cracklin Rosie
519 — Imperial Pooh Bear
520 — Ch. Woodrock Fair Shar O'Pride
521 — Starcrest Sunflower
522 — Plainacre's Love and Kisses
523 — Plainacre's O'Anni of Sherman
524 — Ukwong Star Appeal
525 — Plainacre's Shady Lady
526 — Ch. Claymont's First Noel of Bar-Jo
527 — Starcrest Mr. Broadway
528 — Joshka Creek Wilson
529 — B-Chuzy's Mai Toi Ming
530 — Taibel Texas Tiger of Ukwong
531 — Ch. Hillapao Grand Prix of Pinewood
532 — Redcloud Really Nifty
533 — Ch. Foon Ying Famous Amos
534 — Taichung Dark Design
535 — Ch. Wah-Hu's Black Marble
536 — Sunburst's Lil Luv O'Sompin
537 — Tag-El's Sweetheart Of Jes-Don's
538 — Ch. Leatherwood Casey
539 — Woodrock Jim-Hi
540 — Cherie's Prince Charming
541 — Flowerdrum Song
542 — Laur-Doll Brandy Ling
543 — Ch. Chinabear Aja
544 — Starcrest Lord Hank
545 — Kamara Tiny Bubbles
546 — Shanghai's Eni Meeny Mighty Moe
547 — Dychow Royal Flush Tu
548 — Ch. Joysun Butcherblock
549 — Ch. Sharbo Belcase
550 — Sharbo Blue Mist
551 — Lodiak's Pandora of Charlin
552 — Ch. Charlin's Teja's Stud
553 — Plainacre's Ginger Sparkle
554 — Ch. Hardcastle's Picture Perfect
555 — Fan-C Charm'n Charly J
556 — Ch. Bar Cross Flam'Beau Starr
557 — Sangate's Stardust
558 — Ruby Lynn's Classy of Ursidae
559 — Ch. Lionlair Sgt Pepperland
560 — Redcloud Amber
561 — Redcloud Apple Annie
562 — Cheech Yow Kit
563 — Mister Bear's Mechia
564 — Ch. Su-K's Cowboy By Bearfoot

565 — Koby's Doll-Lee Lin
566 — Bay Bee Chong
567 — Ch. Chinabear Gillian
568 — Dragonwyck Moody Blue
569 — Luvchow's Boson's Mate
570 — Blue Chip Boy of Chia Hsi
571 — Jen-Sen's Black Magic of Palm
572 — Karpar Khanchu
573 — Autumn Sun Sugar Frosted
574 — Heide Seek
575 — Candy Kisses of Chia Hsi
576 — Wild Flower of Chia Hsi
577 — Sangate's T'Son Chia Pao
578 — Charmar Chin Chan Shih of SH
579 — Shei Lai Chun-Kai Tu
580 — Redcloud Blossom Deary
581 — Ch. Koby's Muna Ling
582 — Ch. Koby's Uba Ja
583 — Koby's Miko of Mang Ti
584 — Redcloud Sylvan Razbeary
585 — Shei-Lai's Megan Sunshine
586 — Genghis Khan of Shagg Bark
587 — Ch. Wu-Li's Redcloud Knock Out
588 — Pinewood's Plan-P
589 — Tamarin Blythe Spirit
590 — Tamarin Black Magic
591 — U'Kwong Velvet Touch
592 — Ch. Charkay's Chivas Regal O'Jen Lu
593 — Ch. Ken Chi Pooh Bear
594 — Ch. Al De Bear Kuuipo Ua Lanni, C.D.
595 — Carolanda's Busy Bee
596 — Thelma's Sugar Bear
597 — Ch. Shagg Bark's Sassafras Tea
598 — Redcloud Mulberry, C.D.
599 — Ke-Yo-Ke's Shanghi Girl
600 — Ch. Sundance Liu Hsing Jen Shu
601 — Ch. Autumn Sun Tai Ping
602 — Ch. B-Chuzy's Kodi
603 — Russell's Tahsha Maui
604 — Ch. Janvan Canton Blu-Manchu
605 — Janvan Jes-Don Lookin' Sharp
606 — Ch. Westchow's Ky-Lee Red Don Wan
607 — Ch. Robinhill Antares
608 — Ch. Silverstone's Samoa
609 — Ch. Chi Debut's Nutcracker Suite
610 — Ch. Chi Debut's Metz's Sue Ellen
611 — Silverstone's Noble
612 — Ch. Wow Wow

613 — Shei Lai Little Bit O'Palm
614 — Ch. Sam-Des Roddie's Satisfied
615 — Charkay's Tanqueray
616 — Mane Street's Lady Shanook
617 — Picasso's Jade Buddha
618-T — Tonapah's Ice Tea Rose
619 — Cassanova's Chowder
620 — Buda's Mr. Chips of Rodon
621 — Ch. Rodon's Colonel Casey
622 — Tai Chung Robin O'Cedar Creek
623 — Ch. Tamarin Midday Idol
624 — Campet's E-Lin China Doll
625 — Ch. Shei-Lai Billion Dollar Baby
626 — Shei-Lai Little Char-Lee
627 — Shei-Lai Little Cindy-Lea
628 — Kim's Ginger Bear
629 — Tamarin Mahogany
630 — Bridgewater's Chu Bear
631 — Ch. Coronet's Puttin' On The Ritz
632 — Cedar Creek's Ciji
633 — Wah-Hu Redcloud Apple Bette
634 — Wu-Li's Somethin' Elsa
635 — Ch. Taichung Samantha
636 — Ch. Claymont's Litany
637 — Yew-Tee of St. Noel
638 — Ch. Redcloud Sylvan Sky Walker
639 — Ch. Koby's Smudgy Son
640 — Chi Debut's Gold Dust
641 — Ch. Daystar Orion of Sunny Oak
642 — Ch. Woodside's Tantalizin' Tara
643 — Ch. Autumn Sun Shining Softly
644 — Autumn Sun Gentle Dragon
645 — Ch. Kamara Molly-O
646 — Ch. Redcloud Sylvan Sweet Stuff
647 —
648 — Ch. Mi-Pao's Trademark
649 — Ch. Lallipup's Legend of Lorraine, C.D.
650 —
651 —
652 — Ch. Shilar's Mi Ti Zeus
653 — Ch. Rebelrun's Scarlet Starlet
654 — Ch. Cedar Creek's Jokers Wild
655 — Ukwong Delamere
656 — Courtney's China Star
657 — CC's Blackberry Brandy
658 — Ch. Ter-Bear of Biddles
659 — Quillin's Lien Hua K'al Hua
660 — Ch. Chinabear Golden Kamay

661 — Ch. Chinabear Goodtime Charlie
662 — Ch. Chinabear Shadow Dancer
663 — Ch. Chinabear All Jazzed Up, C.D.
664 — Ch. Ukwong Winter Jasmine
665 — Palm's Mister Sir Sandi
666 — Ch. Redcloud Tug of War
667 — Sheelba Midnight Lotus
668 — B-Chuzy Teddy Bear N'Black
669 — Janvan Extra Special
670 — Ukwong King Cole
671 — Ch. CC's Hon-E-Bear of Carol's
672 — Beekay's Hou Ah Kum
673 — Koby's Precious Susu
674 — Lady Jennifer Letherwood
675 — Jung's Strawberry Stencil
676 — Ch. Ho Yam of Kensington
677 — Miet Su's Fu Chow
678 — Teabear's Blu Plate Special
679 — Lady Lucifer of Chia Hsi
680 — Ch. Rebelrun's Dreamer For Sal Mae
681 — Ch. Mang Ao Ante Up
682 — Luvchow's Oh-Boy It's Chips Ahoy
683 — Cedar Creek's Emperial Tu Tang
684 — Cedar Creek's Tootsie Roll
685-T — Ch. Jen-Lu's Peking Taipan
686 — Wah-Hu's Amelia Bearhart
687 — Silverstone's Madrona
688 — Lli Haven's Ninjitsu
689 — Bear Ritz Shantungs Cinnabar
690 — J'Hay's Mah-Jong
691 — Tarbet's Honey Bear
692 — Checkmate's R-U-Red-E
693 — Pei-Gan Mystery
694 — Ch. Pei-Gan Maxim of Redcloud
695 — Redcloud Candy Apple
696-T — Sunswept Singular Promise
697 — Ch. Coronet Smokin' Joe
698 — My Sweet Harmony
699 — Pepperland Midnight Dreamer
700 — Suika Sang
701 — Sin-Di's Scarlett Harlot
702-T — Kamara Huka Taj
703 — Kuro Kuma of Chia Hsi
704 — Quillen's Queen of Hearts
705-T — Cedar Creek's Prince Charming
706 — Ch. Sundance Kiss'N Tell
707 — Wah-Hu's Obi-Wan Kenobi
708 — The Dove's Magichow, C.D.

709 — Ch. Sam-Des Pure Pleasure Bear
710 — Ch. Pineacre's Honeysuckle Rose
711 — Ch. Campbell's Sergeant Pepper
712 — Ming Chueh Mei
713 — Boblu Star of Palm
714 — Robinhill Sun Shadow
715 — Mang-Ao Bordello Blue of Palm
716 — Leatherwood Jo Anna
717 — Ch. Frelin Hel-Lo Orion
718 — Ch. Charkay's Jack Daniels
719 — Canton Rhapsody In Blue
720 — Ch. Leatherwood Matthew
721 — Man-Kou S'Su Chen Kang
722 — Clarcastle Chang Too Tai
723 — Lioning Ebony Echo
724 — J'Hay's Ebony Empress
725 — Jen-Sen's Polka of Palm
726 — Ch. Robinhill Captain Preppie
727 — War-Rah's Chun Chu Foo
728 — Cedar Creeks Amos Moses
729 — Robinhill Poppycake
730 — We-Ja's Sucette
731 — Ch. Windy Acres Cedar O'Boy
732 — Ch. Imperial Encore
733 — Ch. Dav-Lyn's Akai Chan Fugin
734 — Ch. Carol's Extra Terrific
735 — Ming Ti Shihikachwang
736 — Silverstone's Cameo Jetta
737 — Lioning Choir Boy
738 — Coronet Shenanigans
739 — Wang Poo
740 — Crimson Comet of Lorraine
741 — Jeanette of Kamara
742 — Ch. Imperial Phu Bon
743 — Cedar Creek's Su Zee
744 — Ukwong Another Picture
745 — Sook Loy
746 — Ch. Robinhill Kricket of Tu-Ka's
747 — Ch. Cherie's Mahogany Girl of SH
748 — Van Wa's Dutchess
749 — Silverstone's Victoria
750 — Dychow Terra Tonya Tu
751 — Shebo Rees Kuay Leh
752 — Ch. Koby's Konstant Komment
753 — Plainacre's Little Sir Echo
754 — Westchow's Miss Aster
755 — Ch. Goodtyme's Pac Man
756 — Ch. Chinabear Manolete

757 — Ch. Moonwynd Abracadabra
758-T — Mi-Pao's Woodstock
759 — Ch. Sher-Ron's Susie-Q
760 — Caron's QT of Crescendo
761 — Ch. Quasi of Kamara
762 — Ch. Sunstar's Crunchy Boo Boo Too
763 — Cinnabar's Cotten Jenny
764 — Cedar Creek's Jasmine
765 — Ch. Chinabear Midnite Centurion
766 — Ch. Jen-Lu's Cantankerous O'Sherron
767 — Stacey's Susie Queue
768 — Sundance Hai Li Yung Shu
769 — Ch. Moonwynd After Midnight
770 — Sta-Cee's Dixie Sunshine
771 — Ch. Chinabear Champagne Bubbles
772 — Elsa Lokelani
773 — Ch. Ky-Lee's Strawberry Shortcake
774 — Cedar Creek's Casey Jones
775 — Ch. Tai-Ling's Joy To Biddles
776 — Ch. Sweetkins My-Sam's Great Khan
777 — Rebelrun's Mister Majestic
778 — Lo-Sai's Ching Tssu Ming
779 — Ch. Kitt's Link-A-Yantzee
780 — Wah-Hu Redcloud Legacy of Joy
781 — Ch. Charkay Cherry Marnier
782 — Leatherwood Shannara
783 — Briarwood Squeaki Blue Jeans
784 — Ch. Koby's Spanky
785 — Ch. B & B's Tony The Charmer
786 — Crider's Ming Liu Ching
787 — Ch. Bearfoot's Johnny Reb of Su-K
788 — Koala-Me's Samantha
789 — Woodrock Raider
790 — Kaulee's Kiwi
791 — Al De Bear Hustler's Delilah
792 — Silverstone's Canton Nightcap
793 — Ch. Mister Bear's Wun Sun Tu
794 — Ch. Mister Bear's Fancy Pants
795-T — Ch. Bu Dynasty The Judgement
796 — Lazy Jr's Denim 'n Diamonds
797 — Ch. Taichung Justin Of Mike-Mar
798 — Ch. Janora's Sherpa Khabachen
799 — Pink Lemonade of Chia Hsi
800 — Woodrock Dutch Dream
801 — Imperial Cadenza Los-Cerros
802 — Shanghai's Stoney of Kitts
803 — Ch. Chi-Debut's Iddy Bit of Shang
804 — Ch. Teabear Blueberry Betty

805 — Ch. Cedar Creek's Play Pretty
806 — Ken Lee's Dan De Lion
807 — Ch. Jewell's Friendship of Su-K
808 — Ch. Robinhill Amelia Bearheart
809 — Lum-Li's Coco
810 — Bu Dynasty La Belle Shannah
811 — Ch. Wah-Hu Angel Of The Morning
812 — Taichung Quincy
813 — Cherie's Spartan
814 — Sunstar's Adrian
815 — Bu Dynasty's Metz's Machine
816 — Brer Bear Bosephus
817 — Koby's Princess Elicia
818 — Zeus Xiong Gou of Lambert
819 — Charlin Little Bit of Class
820 — Ch. Redcloud Sylvan Goldy Locks
821-T — Elsa's Hot Cross Buns
822 — Woodrock Pride Piper
823 — Leatherwood Dark Markie
824 — Ch. Bar Cross Sophie Tucker
825 — Ch. Sharbo Mister Cuddly Duddley
826 — Ch. Last Tango of Kamara
827 — Chinabear Kandi Kisses
828 — Sal Mae's Morning Glory
829 — Ral-Lin's Saba Spice
830 — Lady Chiling of Axelson
831 — Ral-Lin's Fantome
832 — Lo Chow's Maggie Hits Town
833 — Pandee's Myra
834 — Bearfoot's Storm A Bru'n
835 — Mariko Suki
836 — Ch. Sing-Fu's The Canadian
837 — B-Chuzy Admiration
838 — Frelin's Madame Mystic Gold
839 — Elsa Be Bare
840 — Coronet's Blythe Spirit
841 — Ch. Coronet's Count On Me
842 — Redcloud Sylvan Tiger Lilly
843 — Baybeary Sylvan Pollywog
844 — Ch. Lov-Chow's Prince Andres
845 — Sal Mae's The Witches Delight
846 — Pine Acre's Desiree
847 — Darkstar Dragonwyck's Knight
848 — Sonlit Dutch Treat
849 — B-Chuzy Kuma's A Pretty Girl
850 — Taichung Chocolate Chip
851 — Ch. Jade West's Golden Boy
852 — Chinabear Strictly Tabu

853 — Kichako Happy Fella
854 — Imperial Tahha
855 — Madame Bolane
856 — Ch. Cambellyn's Eulogy To Surmount
857 — Ky-Lin Panache
858 — Windsong's Rocky Mountain Gem
859 — Nikkie Hsiung Kou Chu-Lyn, C.D.
860 — Cedar Creek's Country Cherub
861 — Janora's Miseltoe
862 — Beijing Blue of China
863 — Al De Bear Zorro of Big Pine
864 — Ch. Proveaux's Quiche Victoria
865 — Moonwynd Dixie Doodle
866 — Ch. Rebelun's Daddy's Girl
867 — Autumnsun Littlest Angel
868 — Wah-Hu's Red Hot Samson
869 — Ch. Wan Cheng's Red Razzbear
870 — Palm's Bandit
871 — Criscoken Mister Wuf
872 — Chia Hsi Sparkling Burgandy
873 — Capehorn's Admiral Rebelrun
874 — Sunburst's Som'r Love
875 — Gemini Star Commander
876 — Ch. Leatherwood Tyrell Sackett
877 — Wah-Hu's Charkay's X-mas Cheer
878 — Ch. Cierra's Lancer
879 — Al De Bear Saucy Sox
880 — Jung's Ricci Kutchina
881 — Barjo's Hot Gossip
882 — Ch. B-Chuzy's Center Fold
883 — Luci Mei Ross B-Chuzy
884 — Coronet Redcloud Bliss-Fully
885 — Koby's Klass Act
886 — Pepperland Truly Scrumptious
887 — Ch. Brigadoon's I'M Fancy Too
888 — Taichung Ahso Pillowtalk
889 — Chow A La Crem Shei Lai
890 — Liontamer Red Cloud Bear Ritz
891 — La Four's Knight Rider
892 — Koby's Utopia of CMDR.
893 — Cierra's Silver Lace
894 — Ch. Meadow's Blackjac O'Starcrest
895 — China Gate China Beauty
896 — Ch. Barjo's Hot Chocolate
897 — Chia Hsi Oriental Poppy
898 — Chinabear Miraculous Mandarin
899 — Shi-Lar's Intimidator
900 — Ch. Canton Cordon Bleu

901 — Ch. Shanghai's Jacoby
902 — Ch. Lady Day of Kamara
903 — Rebelrun Timin It Right
904 — Melody's Maggie O'Ricksha
905 — Chin-Di Dancing Chubbette
906 — Ch. Biddles Tia-Ling Dresden Toi
907 — Ch. Mike-Mar's Hillcrest Pride
908 — Liontamer Lainie Of Palm
909 — Jen-Lu's Tara Te
910 — E. Bear's Sugar
911 — Capote
912 — Biddle's Echo of Solo
913 — Shen-Mi-Te-Wan-Ying
914 — Sal Mae's Love Is The Answer
915 — Ch. Charkay's Gallant Victor
916 — La Four's Red Dynasty
917 — Cedar Creek's Moonshine Runner
918 — Medley's Broncos Legacy
919 — Sing-Fu's Dante of Dragonfire
920 — Coronet Bis-Quette
921 — Ch. Robinhill Charles Lindbear
922 — Ch. Koby's Josie Posie
923 — Kira III
924 — Ch. Koby's Tiffany of Tori
925 — Ch. Koby's Brighton Blue of Kamara
926 — Ch. B-Chuzy Rocky Mountain High
927 — Sunburst's Sugar Cookie
928 — Lioning Romanite
929 — Ch. Lioning Wrinkles
930 — Ch. Rebelrun The Californian
931 — Fort Knox Tequila Sunrise
932 — Lin Su Pebbles of Sunnyoak
933 — Ch. Fat Chance of Kamara
934 — Tamarin Red Velvet Foon Ying
935 — Tia-Ling's Ter-Mara
936 — Davis's Sugartown Express
937 — Ch. Ebony Mist of Prairie View
938 — Robinhill Jolly Guy of Tu-Ka's
939 — Autumn Sun The Rose
940 — Ch. Mister Bear's Devilish Lady M
941 — Redcloud Estyn's China Amber
942 — Valentino's Puka Bear
943 — Mi-Tu's TNT
944 — Ch. Moonshine's Nutcracker
945 — Ch. Ahso Fan-C Warlord of Breezy
946 — Wyndy Acres Ebony Empress
947 — Choi Oi Moriah
948 — Leatherwood Periwinkle Blue

949 — Redcloud Silk Kite
950 — Foonying Star of Wan Cheng
951 — Ch. Koby's Cinnamon Amanda
952 — Taichung Tabatha
953 — Ch. Jasam's Magic Dragon
954 — Ch. Lioning Handsome
955 — Wyndy Acres Isusu
956 — Me-Tu-Sh's Bright Magic
957 — Tu-Sh's Sweet Ums
958 — Barjo's Bamboo Rose
959 — Koby Janora Moon Blossom
960 — Goodtymes Pretty Girl Nikki
961 — Ch. Coronet Redcloud Juniper
962 — Sunburst's Autumn Encore
963 — Ch. Coronet's Tailor Maid
964 — Palm's Sugar Pie Honey
965 — Jasam's Skyeanne At Taichung
966 — Taichung Amanda
967 — Jade West's Blu Cheese Kate
968 — J'Hay's Asian Amber
969 — Ch. Sunburst's Ginger Snap
970 — Sunburst's Echo In Autumn
971 — Jenlu's Gypsy Rose
972 — Redcloud All The Tea In China
973 — Penrik's Strawberry
974 — Redcloud Estyn's Confucius
975 — Jen-Sen's Cream De Cody O'Palm
976 — Ch. Wah-Hu's Redcloud Archangel
977 — Candylion Mai Tai
978 — Cumberland's Morning Star
979 — Taichung's Cumberland Ka-Mai
980 — Carol's Cadillac of Biddles
981 — Coronet's Ebony Taboo
982 — Tu-Sha's Tiger
983 — Wyndy Acres Blue Dunbar
984 — Koby's Canton Cotillion
985 — Ch. Mi-Pao's Ginger
986 — Wingwood Mi Sheba
987 — Sharbo Capsicum
988 — Hoffmann's Tiffany Palm
989 — Mar-Al's Charlie Chan
990 — Souki
991 — Samson Of Israel
992 — Sing Fu's Fadora
993 — Brewer's Di Amore
994 — Redcloud Coronet Mumbo Jumbo
995 — Ch. Sing-Fu's Faleen
996 — Jung's Miss Congeniality

997 — Ch. Robinhill Lucia Manda
998 — Janvan's Miss Ivy League
999 — Cassanova's Harvey Wallbanger
1000 — Silverstone's Heather Angel
1001 — Lioning Mysticia
1002 — Tia-Ling's Silver Chalice
1003 — Mariko Sama of Izumi Farm
1004 — Janvan Princeton O'Tonapah
1005 — Ch. Dandylion Kahlua'N Cream
1006 — Imagine Penny Lane
1007 — Sing-Fu's Suelynn
1008 — Eastside's Barie Son of Kazzan
1009 — Tamarin Chino of Greenpoint
1010 — Ch. Chinabear Caraway
1011 — Ch. Jung's Balboa
1012 — Cariaso's Barnaby of Justin
1013 — Cedar Creek's Sassy Lila
1014 — Ch. Robinhill Amaryllis
1015 — Chinabear Double Delight
1016 — Dandylion Amaretto
1017 — Robinhill Rose of Woodside
1018 — Biddles April Love
1019 — Ch. Biddles Ceje
1020 — Cassanova's Chad
1021 — Toffee Silva
1022 — Chuang Kou
1023 — Paradox's Antigo Canadian Mist
1024 — Jen-Lu Razzle Dazzle O'Cuddly
1025 — Chi Ming Prim And Proper
1026 — Van-Wa's Kisska Supreme
1027 — Ch. Redcloud Sylvan Adam of Eden
1028 — Ch. Ahso Fan-C Ho-Hum O Sampan
1029 — Ch. Checkmate's Soft Parade
1030 — Ch. Koby Kagneys
1031 — Cassanova's Jordache
1032 — Charkay's Amaretto N'Coffee
1033 — Ch. Kobys Ashley of Ricksha
1034 — Ch. Palm's Boogie Woogie Boy
1035 — Westchow's Black Velvet
1036 — Ch. Koby's Pebbles
1037 — Woodside's Hoosier Hero
1038 — Ch. Biddles Chichi of Lang Kou
1039 — Muffin
1040 — Teabear Summerthyme Blues
1041 — Autumn Sun Roses N Ruffles
1042 — Ch. Sunswept's Against The Wind
1043 — Cassanova's Monet Danielle
1044 — Ch. Chia Hsi Go For The Gold

1045 — Ch. Liontamer High Performance
1046 — Elsa's Nuffy of Rosemary
1047 — Foon Ying Morningstar Magic
1048 — Ch. Rebelrun's Bobby Dazzler
1049 — Tai Haven Joy O'McTavish
1050 — Al De Bear Ray of Sunshine
1051 — Coronet's Fringe Benefits
1052 — Silverstone's Canton Rebecca
1053 — Sunny Oak Michelob of Car-Le-On
1054 — Touchtone's Turbo Charged
1055 — Tia-Ling's Angel
1056 — Redcloud Sylvan Song
1057 — Canton Diana
1058 — Tai Haven Mr. McWonderful
1059 — Peewee Chow Sun Guerzon
1060 — Cherie's Kinu Cinnabear Flame
1061 — Redcloud Sylvan Sorta Beary
1062 — Cervan's Flaming Star
1063 — Ch. Roddie's Crown Royal Rainbow
1064 — Lan-Chu's Mystic Angel
1065 — Elite's Blackmale O'Westchow
1066 — Wiz Morgan Faichow LaFour
1067 — Ver-Mar May Ling
1068 — Meadows Reflections of Lady
1069 — Canton Hugger Mugger
1070 — Rebel Runs Emperor Mouti
1071 — Ts'ung Lin's Dragon Lady
1072 — Red Cloud Candy Angel O'Cherie
1073 — Ch. Chinabear Gold Enchantress
1074 — Remital Prinz
1075 — Remital China Doll Mahojongg
1076 — Duke Winchester
1077 — Redcloud Sylvan Aurora
1078 — Kloeber's Black Lace Concho
1079 — Koby's Ambiance of Tori
1080 — Trapper Joe Grizzley Bear
1081 — Versaw's Bashful Dreamer
1082 — Wah-Hu Redcloud Arial
1083 — Lin Su Roses Are Red
1084 — Sylvan Finally Michael
1085 — Ch. Rebelrun's Southern Comfort
1086 — Tai Havens Solitary Man
1087 — Jung's Modern Day Warrior
1088 — Robinhill Sweet William
1089 — Denmar's Diamond Scheton
1090 — Goodytymes Champayne N Silk
1091 — Lin Su Sir Carter Tuf Stuff
1092 — Imagine Tamarin Gold Velvet